Alternate Exercises and Problems

for use with

Intermediate Accounting

Third Edition

J. David Spiceland
University of Memphis

James F. Sepe
Santa Clara University

Lawrence A. Tomassini
The Ohio State University

Prepared by
J. David Spiceland
James F. Sepe

McGraw Hill Irwin

Boston   Burr Ridge, IL   Dubuque, IA   Madison, WI   New York   San Francisco   St. Louis
Bangkok   Bogotá   Caracas   Kuala Lumpur   Lisbon   London   Madrid   Mexico City
Milan   Montreal   New Delhi   Santiago   Seoul   Singapore   Sydney   Taipei   Toronto

Alternate Exercises and Problems for use with
INTERMEDIATE ACCOUNTING
J. David Spiceland, James F. Sepe, and Lawrence A. Tomassini

Published by McGraw-Hill/Irwin, an imprint of The McGraw-Hill Companies, Inc., 1221 Avenue of the Americas, New York, NY 10020. Copyright © 2001, 2004 by The McGraw-Hill Companies, Inc.
All rights reserved.

2 3 4 5 6 7 8 9 0 QPD/QPD 0 9 8 7 6 5 4 3

ISBN 0-07-253482-6

www.mhhe.com

CONTENTS

Part I: Alternate Exercises and Problems

Chapter

Part II: Solutions

Chapter

Part I

Alternate Exercises
and
Problems

Exercise 1-1
Accrual
accounting

Listed below are several transactions that took place during the first two years of operations for the accounting firm of Haskins and Price.

	Year 1	Year 2
Amounts billed to customers for services rendered	$380,000	$440,000
Cash collected from customers	330,000	450,000
Cash disbursements:		
Payment of rent for two years	60,000	- 0 -
Salaries paid to employees for services rendered during the year	200,000	210,000
Travel	50,000	60,000
Utilities	30,000	50,000

In addition, you learn that the company incurred utility costs of $40,000 in year one, that there were no liabilities at the end of year two, and no anticipated bad debts on receivables.

Required:
1   Calculate the net operating cash flow for years 1 and 2.
2. Prepare an income statement for each year according to the accrual accounting model.
3. Determine the amount of receivables from customers that the company would show on its year 1 and year 2 balance sheets prepared according to the accrual accounting model.

Exercise 1-2
Concepts;
terminology;
conceptual
framework

Listed below are several terms and phrases associated with the FASB's conceptual framework and underlying accounting principles. Pair each item from List A (by letter) with the item from List B that is most appropriately associated with it.

List A	List B
____ 1. predictive value	a. applying the same accounting practices over time
____ 2. relevance	b. record expenses in the period the related revenue is recognized
____ 3. reliability	c. concerns the relative size of an item and its effect on decisions
____ 4. comprehensive income	d. concerns the recognition of revenue
____ 5. materiality	e. along with relevance, a primary decision-specific quality
____ 6. consistency	f. the original transaction value upon acquisition
____ 7. verifiability	g. information is useful in predicting the future
____ 8. matching principle	h. pertinent to the decision at hand
____ 9. historical cost principle	i. implies consensus among different measurers
____ 10. realization principle	j. the change in equity from nonowner transactions

Exercise 1-3
Basic assumptions
and principles

Listed below are several statements that relate to financial accounting and reporting. Identify the basic assumption, broad accounting principle, or pervasive constraint which applies to each statement.

1. IBM provides quarterly financial information to its shareholders.
2. Cisco Corporation amortizes the cost of a patent over the patent's useful life.
3. The Zilog Company depreciates the cost of its equipment rather than the current fair market value of the equipment.
4. The Antiel Corporation included a disclosure note describing a lawsuit it is defending even though the suit has not yet been settled.
5. The Feinstein Corporation records revenue when products are delivered to customers, even though the cash has not yet been received.
6. John Gordon, the sole proprietor of Gordon's Hardware, does not list his personal automobile on the balance sheet of the hardware store.

Exercise 1-4
Basic assumptions
and principles

Identify the basic assumption or broad accounting principle that was violated in each of the following situations.

1. Don Sherwood, a shareholder of the Brady Construction Corporation, has not received a financial statement from the company for over two years.

2. The Diatonics Corporation reported equipment on its balance sheet at fair market value.

3. Holyoke Corporation paid $20,000 for a three-year insurance policy and recorded the entire expenditure as insurance expense.

4. The Acme Appliance Company is involved in a major lawsuit. The company is being sued for $10 million dollars for alleged patent infringement. The company believes the suit is without merit and has not disclosed its existence in its financial statements.

5. The Ravel Company's balance sheet includes assets owned by the company as well as assets of its principal shareholder, Jim Thomas.

6. The Marine Chemical Company recorded revenue for a $50,000 advance payment received from a customer. The customer's order will be shipped next month.

Exercise 2-1
Transaction
analysis

The following transactions occurred during April 2003, for the Unisale Corporation. The company owns and operates a wholesale warehouse.
1. Issued 100,000 shares of common stock in exchange for $800,000 in cash.
2. Purchased equipment at a cost of $60,000. $15,000 cash was paid and a note payable was signed for the balance owed.
3. Purchased inventory on account at a cost of $270,000. The company uses the perpetual inventory system.
4. Credit sales for the month totaled $360,000. The cost of the goods sold was $210,000.
5. Paid $20,000 in rent on the warehouse building for the month of April.
6. Paid $15,000 to an insurance company for comprehensive insurance for a two-year period beginning May 1, 2003.
7. Paid $180,000 on account for the merchandise purchased in 3.
8. Collected $190,000 from customers on account.
9. Recorded depreciation expense of $2,000 for the month on the equipment.

Required:
Analyze each transaction and show the effect of each on the accounting equation for a corporation.
Example:

Assets   =   Liabilities   +   Paid-in Capital   +   Retained Earnings
1. +800,000(Cash)   +800,000(Capital stock)

Exercise 2-2
Journal entries

Prepare general journal entries to record each of the transactions listed in Exercise 2-1.

Exercise 2-3
Debits and credits

Indicate whether a credit will increase (I) or decrease (D) each of the following accounts:

	Increase (I) or Decrease (D)	Account
1.	_____	Accounts receivable
2.	_____	Salary expense
3.	_____	Loss on sale of land
4.	_____	Prepaid insurance
5.	_____	Interest revenue
6.	_____	Common stock
7.	_____	Interest payable
8.	_____	Land
9.	_____	Interest expense
10.	_____	Gain on sale of equipment
11.	_____	Interest expense
12.	_____	Accumulated depreciation
13.	_____	Bad debt expense
14.	_____	Sales revenue

Exercise 2-4
Transaction
analysis; debits
and credits

Some of the ledger accounts for the Southern Lumber Company are numbered and listed below. For each of the November 2003 transactions numbered 1 through 12 below, indicate by account number which accounts should be debited and credited. The company uses the perpetual inventory system. Assume that appropriate adjusting entries were made at the end of October.

(1) Accounts payable	(2) Equipment	(3) Inventory
(4) Accounts receivable	(5) Cash	(6) Supplies
(7) Supplies expense	(8) Prepaid insurance	(9) Sales revenue
(10) Retained earnings	(11) Note payable	(12) Common stock
(13) Interest payable	(14) Rent expense	(15) Wages payable
(16) Cost of goods sold	(17) Wage expense	(18) Interest expense

	Account(s) Debited	Account(s) Credited
Example: Purchased equipment for cash	2	5

1. Paid a cash dividend.
2. Paid insurance for the next six months.
3. Sold goods to customers on account.
4. Purchased inventory for cash.
5. Purchased supplies on account.
6. Paid employees wages for November.
7. Issued common stock in exchange for cash.
8. Collected cash from customers on account
9. Borrowed cash from a bank and signed a note.
10. At the end of November, recorded the amount of supplies that had been used during the month.
11. Paid October's interest on a bank loan.
12. Accrued interest expense for November.

Exercise 2-5
Adjusting entries

Prepare the necessary adjusting entries at December 31, 2003, for the Jasper Company for each of the following situations. Assume that no financial statements were prepared during the year and no adjusting entries were recorded.

1. A two-year fire insurance policy was purchased on August 1, 2003, for $12,000. The company debited prepaid insurance for the entire amount.
2. Depreciation on equipment totaled $20,000 for the year.
3. Employee salaries of $27,000 for the month of December will be paid in early January 2004.
4. On October 1, 2003, the company lent $50,000 to a customer. The customer signed a note that requires principal and interest at 8% to be paid on September 30, 2004.
5. In July, the company purchased supplies for $4,500. The entry was recorded as a debit to supplies expense. Supplies on hand at the end of the year totaled $2,200. No supplies had been previously purchased.

Exercise 2-6
Cash versus accrual accounting; adjusting entries

The Calloway Tennis Ball Company prepares monthly financial statements for its bank. The November 30 and December 31, 2003, balance sheets contained the following account information:

	Nov. 30 Dr.	Nov. 30 Cr.	Dec. 31 Dr.	Dec. 31 Cr.
Supplies	4,000		8,000	
Prepaid rent	10,000		7,000	
Interest payable		7,000		4,000
Unearned rent revenue		4,500		3,000

The following information also is known:
a. The December statement of cash flows reported $6,000 in cash paid for supplies.
b. No rent payments were made in December.
c. The December income statement revealed $2,000 in interest expense.
d. On November 1, 2003, a tenant paid Calloway $6,000 in advance rent for the period November through February. Unearned rent revenue was credited.

Required:
1. What was the amount of supplies expense that appeared in the December income statement?
2. What was the amount of rent expense that appeared in the December income statement?
3. What was the amount of cash paid to the company's creditors for interest during December?
4. What was the amount of rent revenue earned in December? What adjusting entry was recorded at the end of December for unearned rent?

Problem 2-1
Accounting cycle
through unadjusted
trial balance

The Tazmanian Hat Company began business in July 2003. During July, the following transactions occurred:

Jul. 1 Issued common stock in exchange for $1,000,000 cash.
2 Purchased inventory on account for $80,000 (the perpetual inventory system is used).
4 Paid the company's landlord $10,000 for rent for the upcoming year.
10 Sold merchandise on account for $120,000. The cost of the merchandise was $75,000.
15 Borrowed $ 50,000 from a local bank and signed a note. Principal and interest at 10% is to be repaid in one year.
20 Paid employees $15,000 wages for the first half of the month.
24 Paid $50,000 to suppliers for the merchandise purchased on July 2.
26 Collected $60,000 on account from customers.
28 Paid various utility bills of $1,500 for the month of July.
31 Paid $8,000 in insurance for the period August 1, 2003 to October 1, 2004.

Required:
1. Prepare general journal entries to record each transaction. Omit explanations.
2. Post the entries to T-accounts.
3. Prepare an unadjusted trial balance as of July 31, 2003.

Problem 2-2
Adjusting entries

The Salem Bread Company produces and sells various bakery products to restaurants. The company's fiscal year-end is December 31. The unadjusted trial balance as of December 31, 2003, appears below.

Account Title	Debits	Credits
Cash	32,000	
Accounts receivable	85,000	
Prepaid rent	4,000	
Supplies	2,300	
Inventory	80,000	
Equipment	225,000	
Accumulated depreciation - equipment		77,000
Accounts payable		38,000
Wages payable		5,000
Note payable		50,000
Interest payable		- 0 -
Unearned revenue		3,000
Common stock		100,000
Retained earnings		127,300
Sales revenue		256,000
Cost of goods sold	145,000	
Wage expense	62,000	
Rent expense	10,000	
Depreciation expense	- 0 -	
Interest expense	- 0 -	
Supplies expense	3,000	
Miscellaneous expense	8,000	
Totals	656,300	656,300

Information necessary to prepare the year-end adjusting entries appears below.
1. Depreciation on the equipment for the year is $22,000.
2. Wages payable at the end of the month should be $7,000.
3. On April 1, 2003, Salem borrowed $50,000 from a local bank and signed a note. The note requires interest to be paid annually on March 31 at 8%. The principal is due in 5 years.
4. $1,000 of supplies remained on hand at December 31, 2003.
5. In November, a customer paid Salem $3,000 for an order that was delivered in December. The cash received was credited to Unearned revenue. No other customer advances were received during the year.
6. On December 1, 2003, $4,000 rent was paid to the owner of the building. The payment represented rent for December through March 2004, at $1,000 per month.

Required:
Prepare the necessary December 31, 2003, adjusting journal entries.

© The McGraw-Hill Companies, Inc., 2004

EXERCISES

Exercise 3-1
Balance sheet
classification

The following are the typical classifications used in a balance sheet:

a) Current assets   f) Current liabilities
b) Investments and funds   g) Long-term liabilities
c) Property, plant and equipment   h) Paid-in-capital
d) Intangible assets   i) Retained earnings
e) Other assets

Required:
For each of the following balance sheet items, use the letters above to indicate the appropriate classification category. If the item is a contra account (valuation account), place a minus sign before the chosen letter.

1. ____ Note receivable, due in 2 years	10. ____	Inventories
2. ____ Accounts receivable	11. ____	Goodwill
3. ____ Accumulated depreciation	12. ____	Accrued salaries payable
4. ____ Land, in use	13 ____	Accrued interest payable
5. ____ Note payable, due in 10 months	14 ____	Prepaid insurance
6. ____ Interest payable	15. ____	Common stock
7. ____ Note receivable, due in 6 months	16. ____	Equipment
8. ____ Cash equivalents	17. ____	Unearned revenue
9. ____ Investment in ABC Corp., long-term	18. ____	Warranties payable

Exercise 3-2
Balance sheet
preparation

The following is a December 31, 2003, post-closing trial balance for the Curtis Corporation.

Account Title	Debits	Credits
Cash and cash equivalents	70,000	
Accounts receivable	110,000	
Inventories	120,000	
Prepaid insurance	3,000	
Investment in Qualcom stock, short-term	15,000	
Machinery and equipment	230,000	
Accumulated depreciation – machinery and equipment		111,000
Note receivable – long-term	50,000	
Interest receivable, due in 3 months	2,000	
Accounts payable		45,000
Wages payable		10,000
Interest payable		3,000
Bonds payable (due in ten years)		100,000
Common stock		200,000
Retained earnings		131,000
Totals	600,000	600,000

Required:
Prepare a classified balance sheet for Curtis Corporation at December 31, 2003.

Exercise 3-3
Financial
disclosures

The following are typical disclosures that would appear in the notes accompanying financial statements. For each of the items listed, indicate where the disclosure would likely appear — either in (A) the significant accounting policies note, or (B) a separate note.

1. Depreciation method   A
2. Information on related party transactions   ____
3. Method of accounting for acquisitions   ____
4. Composition and details of long-term debt   ____
5. Inventory method   ____
6. Basis of revenue recognition   ____
7. Major damage to a plant facility occurring after year-end   ____
8. Composition of accrued liabilities   ____

Exercise 3-4
Calculating ratios

The year 2003 balance sheet for the Tomassini Corporation is shown below.

Tomassini Corporation
Balance Sheet
December 31, 2003

Assets:	($ in 000s)
Cash	$ 150
Accounts receivable	400
Inventories	500
Property, plant, and equipment (net)	1,200
Total assets	$2,250
Liabilities and Shareholders' Equity:	
Current liabilities	$ 600
Long-term liabilities	500
Paid-in capital	1,000
Retained earnings	150
Total liabilities and shareholders' equity	$2,250

The company's 2003 income statement reported the following amounts ($ in thousands):

Net sales	$6,600
Interest expense	30
Income tax expense	200
Net income	260

Required:
Determine the following ratios for 2003:
a. current ratio
b. acid-test ratio
c. debt to equity ratio
d. times interest earned ratio

Exercise 3-5
Effect of
management
decisions on ratios

Most decisions made by management impact the ratios analysts use to evaluate performance. Indicate (by letter) whether each of the actions listed below will immediately increase (I), decrease (D), or have no effect (N) on the ratios shown. Assume each ratio is less than 1.0 before the action is taken.

Action	Current ratio	Acid-test ratio	Debt to equity ratio
1. Issuance of common stock for cash	_____	_____	_____
2. Purchase of inventory on account	_____	_____	_____
3. Receipt of cash from a customer on account	_____	_____	_____
4. Expiration of prepaid rent	_____	_____	_____
5. Payment of a cash dividend	_____	_____	_____
6. Purchase of equipment with a 6-month note	_____	_____	_____
7. Purchase of long-term investment for cash	_____	_____	_____
8. Sale of equipment for cash (no gain or loss)	_____	_____	_____
9. Write-off of obsolete inventory	_____	_____	_____
10. Decision to refinance on a long-term basis currently-maturing debt	_____	_____	_____

PROBLEMS

Problem 3-1
Balance sheet
preparation

The following is a December 31, 2003, post-closing trial balance for the Alexandria Exploration Corporation.

Account Title	Debits	Credits
Cash	52,000	
Accounts receivable	223,000	
Allowance for uncollectible accounts		15,000
Inventories	200,000	
Supplies	3,000	
Investments	140,000	
Land	100,000	
Buildings	500,000	
Accumulated depreciation - buildings		150,000
Machinery	250,000	
Accumulated depreciation - machinery		80,000
Goodwill (net of amortization)	36,000	
Accounts payable		125,000
Bonds payable		500,000
Interest payable		40,000
Common stock		500,000
Retained earnings		94,000
Totals	1,504,000	1,504,000

Additional information:
1. Accounts receivable includes a $50,000 note receivable received from a customer that is due in 2005. Also included is interest on the note of $3,000 that is due in six months.
2. The land account includes land that cost $20,000 that the company has not used and is currently listed for sale.
3. The investment account includes a $10,000, 3-month certificate of deposit due in 40 days. The remaining investments will be sold within the next year.
4. The bonds payable account consists of the following:
   a. a $200,000 issue due in six months.
   b. a $300,000 issue due in six years.
5. The common stock account represents 500,000 shares of no par value common stock issued and outstanding. The corporation has 1,000,000 shares authorized.

Required:
Prepare a classified balance sheet for Alexandria at December 31, 2003.

Problem 3-2
Balance sheet
preparation

Presented below is the balance sheet for the Tillamoo Cheese Company at December 31, 2003.

Current assets	$ 740,000	Current liabilities	$ 620,000
Investments	300,000	Long-term liabilities	1,000,000
Property, plant and			
equipment	2,450,000	Shareholders' equity	2,170,000
Intangible assets	300,000	Total liabilities and	
Total assets	$3,790,000	shareholders' equity ..	$3,790,000

The captions shown in the summarized statement above include the following:

a. Current assets: cash, $170,000; cash equivalents, $20,000; accounts receivable, $300,000; inventories, $235,000; and prepaid expenses, $15,000.

b. Investments: investments in common stock, short-term, $40,000; investments in bonds of other corporations, long-term, $260,000.

c. Property, plant, and equipment: buildings, $1,200,000 less accumulated depreciation, $300,000; equipment, $900,000 less accumulated depreciation, $300,000; and land, $950,000.

d. Intangible assets: patent, $80,000; and goodwill, $220,000.

e. Current liabilities: accounts payable, $260,000; notes payable, short-term, $180,000, and long-term, $100,000; interest payable, $20,000; and other accrued liabilities, $60,000

f. Long-term liabilities: bonds payable due 2009.

g. Shareholders' equity: common stock, $1,500,000; retained earnings, $670,000.

Required:
Prepare a corrected classified balance sheet for Tillamoo at December 31, 2003.

EXERCISES

Exercise 4-1
Income statement
format; single-step
and multiple-step

The following is a partial trial balance for Apex Computer Corporation as of December 31, 2003:

Account Title	Debits	Credits
Sales revenue		3,400,000
Interest revenue		35,000
Gain on sale of equipment		30,000
Loss from hurricane damage (event is both unusual and infrequent)	300,000	
Cost of goods sold	2,250,000	
Restructuring costs	400,000	
Administrative expense	450,000	
Selling expense	150,000	
Interest expense	20,000	

500,000 shares of common stock were outstanding throughout 2003. Income tax expense has not yet been accrued. The income tax rate is 40%.

Required:
1. Prepare a single-step income statement for 2003, including EPS disclosure.
2. Prepare a multiple-step income statement for 2003, including EPS disclosure.

Exercise 4-2
Discontinued
operations

The Bilibong Company had three distinct operating divisions, each of which qualifies as a separate component. The sports equipment division had been unprofitable, and on June 1, 2003, the company adopted a plan to sell the assets of the division. The actual sale was effected on December 3, 2003, at a price of $1,200,000. The sale resulted in a before-tax gain of $300,000

The division incurred before-tax operating losses of $380,000 from the beginning of the year through December 3. The income tax rate is 40%. Bilibong's after-tax income from its continuing operations is $500,000.

Required:
Prepare an income statement for 2003 beginning with "income from continuing operations." Include appropriate EPS disclosures assuming 200,000 shares of common stock were outstanding throughout the year.

Exercise 4-3
Discontinued
operations;
disposal in a
subsequent year

The Ottoboni Corporation had two operating divisions, one manufacturing division and a finance division. Both divisions are considered separate components. The finance division has been unprofitable, and on October 3, 2003, Ottoboni adopted a formal plan to sell the division. The sale was completed on March 19, 2004. At December 31, 2003, the division was considered held for sale

On December 31, 2003, the company's fiscal year-end, the book value of the assets of the finance division was $2,100,000. On that date, the fair value of the assets, less costs to sell, was $1,900,000. The before-tax operating loss of the division for the year was $270,000. The company's effective tax rate is 40%. The after-tax income from continuing operations for 2003 is $600,000.

Required:
1. Prepare a partial income statement for 2003 beginning with income from continuing operations. Ignore EPS disclosures.
2. Repeat requirement 1 assuming that the estimated net sales price of the finance division's assets was $2,400,000, instead of $1,900,000.

Exercise 4-4
Accounting
change

The Rufus and Cleft Mining Company purchased machinery on June 15, 2001, for $2,500,000. A six-year life was estimated and a salvage value of $100,000 was anticipated. The company decided to use the straight-line depreciation method and recorded $600,000 in depreciation during 2001 and 2002. Early in 2003, the company revised the *total* estimated life of the machinery to 10 years. The estimated salvage value was revised to $200,000.

Required:
1. Briefly describe the accounting treatment for this change.
2. Determine depreciation for 2003.

Exercise 4-5
Statement of cash flows; classifications

The statement of cash flows classifies all cash inflows and outflows into one of the three categories shown below and lettered from a-c. In addition, certain transactions that do not involve cash are reported in the statement as noncash investing and financing activities, labeled d.

 a) Operating activities
 b) Investing activities
 c) Financing activities
 d) Noncash investing and financing activities

Required:

For each of the following transactions, use the letters above to indicate the appropriate classification category.

1. _____ Purchase of equipment in exchange for a note payable.
2. _____ Payment of rent.
3. _____ Collection of cash from customers.
4. _____ Payment of interest on debt.
5. _____ Purchase of a bond of another company.
6. _____ Issuance of common stock for cash.
7. _____ Sale of land for cash.
8. _____ Receipt of interest on a note receivable.
9. _____ Receipt of principal on a note receivable.
10. _____ Payment of cash dividends to shareholders.
11. _____ Payment to suppliers of inventory.

PROBLEMS

Problem 4-1
Comparative
income statements;
multiple-step
format

Selected information about income statement accounts for the Ajax Company is presented below for the fiscal year ended December 31, 2003.

Sales	$6,200,000
Cost of goods sold	3,500,000
Administrative and selling expenses	1,500,000

Several events occurred during 2003 that have *not* yet been reflected in the above accounts:

1. A landslide caused $75,000 in uninsured damages to a warehouse. The landslide was considered to be an infrequent but not unusual event.
2. Interest revenue in the amount of $100,000 was earned.
3. The company sold some property in Alaska that it had been holding for 20 years. The sale resulted in a gain of $2 million. The company has no other investments in land and the transaction was considered to be both unusual and infrequent
4. The company incurred restructuring costs of $250,000
5. Interest expense on debt totaled $150,000.
6. Equipment was sold for a loss of $40,000.

Required:
Prepare a multiple-step income statement for the Ajax Company for the year 2003, including income taxes computed at 40%. Ignore EPS disclosures.

Problem 4-2
Discontinued
operations

The following condensed income statements of the Huntington Steel Corporation are presented for the two years ended December 31, 2003 and 2002:

	2003	2002
Sales	$20,000,000	$19,600,000
Cost of goods sold	13,400,000	13,200,000
Gross profit	6,600,000	6,400,000
Operating expenses	2,700,000	2,600,000
Operating income	3,900,000	3,800,000
Gain on sale of division	800,000	--
	4,700,000	3,800,000
Income tax expense	1,880,000	1,520,000
Net income	$2,820,000	$2,280,000

On September 6, 2003, Huntington entered into an agreement to sell the assets of one of its divisions. The division comprises operations and cash flows that can be clearly distinguished, operationally and for financial reporting purposes, from the rest of the company. The division was sold on December 31, 2003, for $7,000,000. Book value of the division's assets was $6,200,000. The division's contribution to Huntington's operating income before-tax for each year was as follows:

2003	$455,000 loss
2002	$325,000 income

Assume an income tax rate of 40%.

Required:
1. Prepare revised income statements according to generally accepted accounting principles, beginning with income from continuing operations before income taxes. Ignore EPS disclosures.
2. Assume that by December 31, 2003, the division had not yet been sold but was considered held for sale. The fair value of the division's assets on December 31 was $7,000,000. How would the presentation of discontinued operations be different from your answer to requirement 1?
3. Assume that by December 31, 2003, the division had not yet been sold but was considered held for sale. The fair value of the division's assets on December 31 was $5,000,000. How would the presentation of discontinued operations be different from your answer to requirement 1?

Exercise 5-1
Installment sales;
alternative
recognition
methods

On June 1, 2003, the Luttman and Dowd Company sold inventory to the Ushman Corporation for $400,000. Terms of the sale called for a down payment of $100,000 and four annual installments of $75,000 due on each June 1, beginning June 1, 2004. Each installment also will include interest on the unpaid balance applying an appropriate interest rate. The inventory cost Foster $150,000. The company uses the perpetual inventory system.

Required:

1. Compute the amount of gross profit to be recognized from the installment sale in 2003, 2004, 2005, 2006, and 2007 using point of delivery revenue recognition. Ignore interest charges.
2. Repeat requirement 1 applying the installment sales method.
3. Repeat requirement 1 applying the cost recovery method.

Exercise 5-2
Construction
accounting;
percentage-of-
completion and
completed contract
methods

The Ugenti Construction Company contracted to construct a warehouse building for $2,600,000. Construction began in 2003 and was completed in 2004. Data relating to the contract are summarized below:

	2003	2004
Costs incurred during the year	$ 360,000	$1,650,000
Estimated costs to complete as of 12/31 .	1,560,000	-
Billings during the year	430,000	2,130,000
Cash collections during the year..............	320,000	2,280,000

Required:

1. Compute the amount of gross profit or loss to be recognized in 2003 and 2004 using the percentage-of-completion method.
2. Compute the amount of gross profit or loss to be recognized in 2003 and 2004 using the completed contract method.
3. Prepare a partial balance sheet to show how the information related to this contract would be presented at the end of 2003 using the percentage-of completion method.
4. Prepare a partial balance sheet to show how the information related to this contract would be presented at the end of 2003 using the completed contract method.

Exercise 5-3
Percentage-of-completion
method; loss
projected on entire
project

On April 13, 2003, the Pagano Construction Company entered into a three-year construction contract to build a mall for a price of $12,000,000. During 2003, costs of $3,000,000 were incurred with estimated costs of $6,000,000 yet to be incurred. Billings of $3,800,000 were sent and cash collected was $3,250,000.

In 2004, costs incurred were $4,000,000 with remaining costs estimated to be $5,600,000. 2004 billings were $3,500,000 and $3,600,000 cash was collected. The project was completed in 2005 after additional costs of $5,800,000 were incurred. The company's fiscal year-end is December 31. Arrow uses the percentage-of-completion method.

Required:
1. Calculate the amount of gross profit or loss to be recognized in each of the three years.
2. Prepare journal entries for 2003 and 2004 to record the transactions described (credit "Various accounts" for construction costs incurred).
3. Prepare a partial balance sheet to show the presentation of the project as of December 31, 2003 and 2004.

Exercise 5-4
Franchise sales;
revenue
recognition

On November 15, 2003, the Coldstone Ice Cream Company entered into a franchise agreement with an individual. In exchange for an initial franchise fee of $25,000, Coldstone will provide initial services to the franchisee to include assistance in design and construction of the building, help in training employees, help in obtaining financing, and management advice over the first five years of the ten-year franchise agreement.

50% of the initial franchise fee is payable on November 15, 2003, with the remaining $12,500 payable in five equal annual installments beginning on November 15, 2004. These installments will include interest at an appropriate rate. The franchise opened for business on February 15, 2004.

Required:
Assume that the initial services to be performed by Coldstone subsequent to November 15, 2003, are substantial and that collectibility of the installment receivable is reasonably certain. Substantial performance of the initial services is deemed to have occurred when the franchise opened. Prepare the necessary journal entries for the following dates (ignoring interest charges):

1. November 15, 2003, and
2. February 15, 2004.

Intermediate Accounting, 3/e

Exercise 5-5
Evaluating
efficiency of asset
management

The year 2003 income statement of Garret & Sons Music Company reported net sales of $10 million, cost of goods sold of $6 million, and net income of $1 million. The following table shows the company's comparative balance sheets for 2003 and 2002:

	($ in 000s)	
Assets:	**2003**	**2002**
Cash	$ 240	$ 280
Accounts receivable	800	600
Inventory	850	700
Property, plant, and equipment (net)	2,600	2,520
Total assets	$4,490	$4,100
Liabilities and Shareholders' Equity:		
Current liabilities	$ 720	$ 650
Notes payable	600	1,000
Paid-in capital	2,000	2,000
Retained earnings	1,170	450
Total liabilities and shareholders equity	$4,490	$4,100

Some industry averages for the company's line of business are:

inventory turnover	6	times
average collection period	28	days
asset turnover	2	times

Required:

Assess Garret & Son's asset management relative to its industry.

Exercise 5-6
Profitability ratios

The following condensed information was reported by Sanders Manufacturing, Inc. for 2003 and 2002:

	($ in 000s)	
	2003	**2002**
Income statement information:		
Net sales	$7,200	$6,800
Net income	360	408
Balance Sheet information:		
Current assets	$ 800	$ 750
Property, plant, and equipment (net)	2,100	1,950
Total assets	$2,900	$2,700
Current liabilities	$ 250	$ 400
Long-term liabilities	950	750
Paid-in capital	1,000	1,000
Retained earnings	700	550
Liabilities and shareholders' equity	$2,900	$2,700

Required:
1. Determine the following ratios for 2003:
   a. profit margin on sales
   b. return on assets
   c. return on shareholders' equity
2. Determine the amount of dividends paid to shareholders during 2003.

Problem 5-1
Installment sales;
alternative
recognition
methods

On October 31, 2003, the Dionne Company sold merchandise to the Parker Corporation for $800,000. Terms of the sale called for a down payment of $200,000 and three annual installments of $200,000 due on each October 31, beginning October 31, 2004. Each installment also will include interest on the unpaid balance applying an appropriate interest rate. The book value of the merchandise on Dionne's books on the date of sale was $400,000. The perpetual inventory system is used. The company's fiscal year end is December 31.

Required:
1. Prepare a table showing the amount of gross profit to be recognized in each of the four years of the installment sale applying each of the following methods:
   a. Point of delivery revenue recognition.
   b. Installment sales method.
   c. Cost recovery method.
2. Prepare journal entries for each of the four years applying the three revenue recognition methods listed in requirement 1. Ignore interest charges.
3. Prepare a partial balance sheet as of the end of 2003 and 2004 listing the items related to the installment sale applying each of the three methods listed in requirement 1.

Problem 5-2
Percentage-of-
completion method

In the year 2003, the Malinkrodt Construction Company entered into a contract to construct a road for Dade County for $15,000,000. The road was completed in 2005. Information related to the contract is as follows:

	2003	2004	2005
Costs incurred during the year	$4,000,000	$4,800,000	$4,200,000
Estimated costs to complete as of year-end	8,000,000	4,000,000	-
Billings during the year	3,500,000	5,000,000	6,500,000
Cash collections during the year..........	2,800,000	5,600,000	6,600,000

Malinkrodt uses the percentage-of-completion method of accounting for long-term construction contracts.

Required:

1. Calculate the amount of gross profit to be recognized in each of the three years.
2. Prepare all necessary journal entries for each of the years (credit "Various accounts" for construction costs incurred).
3. Prepare a partial balance sheet for 2003 and 2004 showing any items related to the contract.
4. Calculate the amount of gross profit to be recognized in each of the three years assuming the following costs incurred and costs to complete information:

	2003	2004	2005
Costs incurred during the year	$4,000,000	$4,200,000	$7,200,000
Estimated costs to complete as of year-end	8,000,000	7,100,000	-

EXERCISES

Exercise 6-1
Future value;
single amount

Determine the future value of the following single amounts:

		Invested Amount	Interest Rate	No. of Periods
	1.	$50,000	8%	10
	2.	30,000	6	20
	3.	40,000	10	30
	4.	60,000	4	12

Exercise 6-2
Present value;
single amount

Determine the present value of the following single amounts:

		Future Amount	Interest Rate	No. of Periods
	1.	$20,000	8%	10
	2.	10,000	6	20
	3.	25,000	10	30
	4.	40,000	12	8

Exercise 6-3
Present value;
annuities

Using the appropriate present value table and assuming a 10% annual interest rate, determine the present value on December 31, 2003, of a five-period annual annuity of $10,000 under each of the following situations:
1. The first payment is received on December 31, 2004, and interest is compounded annually.
2. The first payment is received on December 31, 2004, and interest is compounded annually.

Exercise 6-4
Solving for
unknowns; single
amounts

For each of the following situations involving single amounts, solve for the unknown (?). Assume that interest is compounded annually. (i = interest rate, and n = number of years)

	Present Value	Future Value	i	n
1.	?	$50,000	8%	10
2.	$31,947	70,000	?	20
3.	9,576	40,000	10	?
4.	20,462	100,000	?	14
5.	15,000	?	6	30

Exercise 6-5
Solving for
unknowns;
annuities

For each of the following situations involving annuities, solve for the unknown (?). Assume that interest is compounded annually and that all annuity amounts are received at the *end* of each period. (i = interest rate, and n = number of years)

	Present Value	Annuity Amount	i	n
1.	?	$ 5,000	10%	10
2.	$298,058	60,000	?	8
3.	337,733	30,000	8	?
4.	600,000	74,435	?	15
5.	200,000	?	12	6

Exercise 6-6
Deferred annuities;
solving for annuity
amount

On June 1, 2003, April Smith purchased carpeting from the Wearwell Carpet Company for $4,800. In order to increase sales, Wearwell allows customers to pay in installments and will defer any payments for 12 months. April will make 18 equal monthly payments, beginning June 1, 2004. The annual interest rate implicit in this agreement is 24%.

Required:

Calculate the monthly payment necessary for April to pay for her purchases.

PROBLEMS

Problem 6-1
Present and Future
Value

The Reuter Company is facing several decisions regarding investing and financing activities. Address each decision independently.

1. On May 31, 2003, Reuter purchased equipment and agreed to pay the vendor $50,000 on the purchase date and the balance in four annual installments of $20,000 on each May 31 beginning May 31, 2004. Assuming that an interest rate of 8% properly reflects the time value of money in this situation, at what amount should Reuter value the equipment?

2. Reuter needs to accumulate sufficient funds to pay a $600,000 debt that comes due on December 31, 2007. The company will accumulate the funds by making four equal annual deposits to an account paying 4% interest compounded annually. Determine the required annual deposit if the first deposit is made on December 31, 2004.

3. Reuter needs to decide whether to lease or buy an office building. The purchase price of the building would be $2,000,000. If the lease option is chosen, the lease agreement would require 20 annual payments of $200,000 beginning immediately. A 10% interest rate is implicit in the lease agreement. Which option, buy or lease, should Reuter choose? Assume zero residual value if the buy option is chosen.

Problem 6-2
Deferred annuities

Smokey Sims is 60 years old and has been asked to accept early retirement from his company. The company has offered three alternative compensation packages to induce Smokey to retire:

1. $400,000 cash payment to be paid immediately.
2. A 15-year annuity of $40,000 beginning immediately.
3. A 15-year annuity of $45,000 beginning at age 65.

Required:

Which alternative should Smokey choose assuming that he is able to invest funds at a 6% rate?

EXERCISES

Exercise 7-1
Trade and cash discounts; the gross method and the net method compared

CCM Corporation, a manufacturer of furnaces, sold 200 units to a customer on April 6, 2003. The units have a list price of $800 each, but the customer was given a 20% trade discount. The terms of the sale were 1/10, n30.

Required:
1. Prepare the journal entries to record the sale on April 6 (ignore cost of goods) and payment on April 16, 2003, assuming that the gross method of accounting for cash discounts is used.
2. Prepare the journal entries to record the sale on April 6 (ignore cost of goods) and payment on May 6, 2003, assuming that the gross method of accounting for cash discounts is used.
3. Repeat requirements 1. and 2. assuming that the *net* method of accounting for cash discounts is used.

Exercise 7-2
Uncollectible accounts; allowance method; balance sheet approach

The Gadzooks Chip Company offers credit terms to its customers. At the end of 2003, accounts receivable totaled $2,223,000. The allowance method is used to account for uncollectible accounts. The allowance for uncollectible accounts had a credit balance of $68,000 at the beginning of 2003 and $46,200 in receivables was written off during the year as uncollectible. No previously written off receivables were collected. The company estimates bad debts by applying a percentage of 3% to accounts receivable at the end of the year.

Required:
1. Prepare journal entries to record the write-off of receivables and the year-end adjusting entry for bad debt expense.
2. How would accounts receivable be shown in the 2003 year-end balance sheet?

Exercise 7-3
Noninterest-bearing note receivable

On March 31, 2003, the Applix Corporation sold some merchandise to a customer for $80,000 and agreed to accept as payment a noninterest-bearing note with a 6% discount rate requiring the payment of $80,000 on March 31, 2004.

Required:
1. Prepare journal entries to record the sale of merchandise (omit any entry that might be required for the cost of the goods sold), the December 31, 2003 interest accrual, and the March 31 collection.
2. What is the *effective* interest rate on the note?

Exercise 7-4
Factoring of
accounts
receivable without
recourse

The Fullbright Book Company transferred $100,000 of accounts receivable to the American Trust Bank. The transfer was made *without recourse*. American Trust remits 90% of the factored amount and retains 10%. When the bank collects the receivables, it will remit to Fullbright the retained amount less a 1% fee (1% of the total factored amount).

Required:
Prepare the journal entry to record the transfer on the books of Fullbright assuming that the sale criteria are met.

Exercise 7-5
Factoring of
accounts
receivable with
recourse

[This is a variation of the previous exercise modified to focus on factoring with recourse.]

The Fullbright Book Company transferred $100,000 of accounts receivable to the American Trust Bank. The transfer was made *with recourse*. American Trust remits 90% of the factored amount and retains 10%. When the bank collects the receivables, it will remit to Fullbright the retained amount less a 1% fee (1% of the total factored amount). Fullbright anticipates a $4,000 recourse obligation.

Required:
Prepare the journal entry to record the transfer on the books of Fullbright assuming that the "sale" criteria are met.

Exercise 7-6
Discounting a note
receivable

The Falletti Pasta Company obtained a $50,000 note receivable from a customer on June 1, 2003. The note, along with interest at 8%, is due on June 1, 2004. On September 1, 2003, Falletti discounted the note at the Bank of Los Alimos. The bank's discount rate is 10%.

Required:
Prepare the journal entries required on September 1, 2003, to accrue interest and to record the discounting (round all calculations to the nearest dollar) for Falletti. Assume that the discounting is accounted for as a sale.

Exercise 7-7
Bank
reconciliation and
adjusting entries
[Based on Appendix]

The Harrison Company maintains a checking account at the Bank of Milwaukee. The bank provides a bank statement along with canceled checks on the last day of each month. The August, 2003 bank statement included the following information:

Balance, August 1, 2003	$ 68,326
Deposits	245,300
Checks processed	(236,222)
Service charges	(50)
NSF checks	(680)
Monthly deposit into savings account deducted directly by bank from account	(2,000)
Balance, August 31, 2003	$ 74,674

The company's general ledger account had a balance of $78,984 at the end of August. Deposits outstanding totaled $8,200 and all checks written by the company were processed by the bank except for those totaling $8,420. In addition, a $2,000 check to a supplier correctly recorded by the bank was incorrectly recorded by the company as a $200 credit to cash.

Required:
1. Prepare a bank reconciliation for the month of August.
2. Prepare the necessary journal entries at the end of August to adjust the general ledger cash account.

Problem 7-1
Uncollectible
accounts;
allowance method;
income statement
and balance sheet
approach

SDLI, Inc. grants its customers 30 days credit. The company uses the allowance method for its uncollectible accounts receivable. During the year, a monthly bad debt accrual is made by multiplying 2% times the amount of credit sales for the month. At the fiscal year-end of December 31, an aging of accounts receivable schedule is prepared and the allowance for uncollectible accounts is adjusted accordingly.

At the end of 2002, accounts receivable were $1,250,000 and the allowance account had a credit balance of $106,000. Accounts receivable activity for 2003 was as follows:

Beginning balance	$1,250,000
Credit sales	3,800,000
Collections	(3,745,000)
Write-offs	(82,000)
Ending balance	$1,223,000

The company's controller prepared the following aging summary of year-end accounts receivable:

	Summary	
Age Group	Amount	Percent Uncollectible
0-60 days	$ 825,000	2%
61-90 days	220,000	10%
91-120 days	50,000	30%
Over 120 days	128,000	40%
Total	$1,223,000	

Required:
1. Prepare a summary journal entry to record the monthly bad debt accrual and the write-offs during the year.
2. Prepare the necessary year-end adjusting entry for bad debt expense.
3. What is total bad debt expense for 2003? How would accounts receivable appear in the 2003 balance sheet?

Problem 7-2
Miscellaneous
receivable
transactions

The Appomatix Company sells fertilizer and pesticides to wholesalers. The company's fiscal year-end is December 31. During 2003, the following transactions related to receivables occurred:

March 31 Sold merchandise to the Misthos Co. and accepted a noninterest-bearing note with a discount rate of 10%. The $12,000 payment is due on March 31, 2004.

April 12 Sold merchandise to Able Co. for $10,000 with terms 2/10, n30. Appomatix uses the gross method to account for cash discounts.

April 21 Collected the entire amount due from Able Co.

April 27 A customer returned merchandise costing Appomatix $6,000. Appomatix reduced the customers receivable balance by $8,000, the sales price of the merchandise. The company records sales returns as they occur.

May 30 Transferred receivables of $100,000 to a factor without recourse. The factor charged Appomatix a 2% finance charge on the receivables transferred. The sale criteria are met.

July 31 Sold merchandise to Favre Corporation for $15,000 and accepted an 8%, 6-month note. 8% is an appropriate rate for this type of note.

Sept. 30 Discounted the Favre Corporation note at the bank. The bank's discount rate is 12%. The note was discounted without recourse.

Required:

1. Prepare the necessary journal entries for Appomatix for each of the above dates. For transactions involving the sale of merchandise, ignore the entry for the cost of goods sold (Round all calculations to the nearest dollar).

2. Prepare any necessary adjusting entries at December 31, 2003. Adjusting entries are only recorded at year-end (Round all calculations to the nearest dollar).

Exercise 8-1
Perpetual and periodic inventory systems compared

The following information is available for the Kleinschmidt Corporation for 2003:

Beginning inventory	$112,000
Merchandise purchases (on account)	265,000
Freight charges on purchases (on account)	16,000
Merchandise returned to supplier (for credit)	6,000
Ending inventory	123,000
Sales (on account)	350,000
Cost of merchandise sold	264,000

Required:
Applying both a perpetual and a periodic inventory system, prepare the journal entries that summarize the transactions that created these balances. Include all end-of-period adjusting entries indicated.

Exercise 8-2
Trade and purchase discounts; the gross method and the net method compared

The Kavendish Company, a manufacturer of commercial-use washing machines, sold 50 units to the E-z Sleep Motel chain on January 14, 2003. The units have a list price of $800 each, but E-z Sleep was given a 25% trade discount. The terms of the sale were 2/10, n30. E-z Sleep uses a periodic inventory system.

Required:
1. Prepare the journal entries to record the purchase by E-z Sleep on January 14 and payment on January 23, 2003, using the gross method of accounting for purchase discounts.
2. Prepare the journal entries to record the purchase on January 14 and payment on February 13, 2003, using the gross method of accounting for purchase discounts.
3. Repeat requirements 1 and 2 using the *net* method of accounting for purchase discounts.

Exercise 8-3
Goods in transit;
consignment

The December 31, 2003, year-end inventory balance of the Delphi Printing Company is $317,000. You have been asked to review the following transactions to determine if they have been correctly recorded.

1. Materials purchased from a supplier and shipped to Delphi f.o.b. destination on December 28, 2003, were received on January 2, 2004. The invoice cost of $50,000 is *not* included in the preliminary inventory balance.
2. At year-end, Delphi had $12,000 of merchandise on consignment from the Harvey Company. This merchandise *is* included in the preliminary inventory balance.
3. On December 29, merchandise costing $17,000 was shipped to a customer f.o.b. shipping point and arrived at the customer's location on January 3, 2004. The merchandise is *not* included in the preliminary inventory balance.
4. Materials purchased from a supplier and shipped to Delphi f.o.b. shipping point on December 28, 2003 were received on January 4, 2004. The invoice cost of $32,000 is *not* included in the preliminary inventory balance.

Required:
Determine the correct inventory amount to be reported on Delphi's 2003 balance sheet.

Exercise 8-4
Inventory cost flow
methods; perpetual
system

The Alpenrose Milk Company uses a *perpetual* inventory system. The following transactions affected its merchandise inventory during the month of March, 2003:

March 1	—	Inventory on hand — 3,000 units; cost $8.00 each.
March 8	—	Purchased 5,000 units for $8.40 each.
March 14	—	Sold 4,000 units for $14.00 each.
March 18	—	Purchased 6,000 units for $8.20 each.
March 25	—	Sold 7,000 units for $14.00 each.
March 31	—	Inventory on hand — 3,000 units.

Required:
Determine the inventory balance Alpenrose would report on its March 31, 2003, balance sheet and the cost of goods sold it would report on its March, 2003, income statement using each of the following cost flow methods:

1. First-in, first-out (FIFO)
2. Last-in, first-out (LIFO)
3. Average cost

Intermediate Accounting, 3/e

Exercise 8-5
Average cost
method; periodic
and perpetual
systems

The following information is taken from the inventory records of the Bauxite Company:

Beginning inventory, 4/1/03   7,000 units @ $22.00
Purchases:
    4/5   6,000 units @ $22.65
    4/26   9,000 units @ $24.00
Sales:
    4/11   5,000 units
    4/28   8,000 units

9,000 units were on hand at the end of April.

Required:
1. Assuming that Bauxite uses a periodic inventory system and employs the average cost method, determine cost of goods sold for April and April's ending inventory.
2. Repeat requirement 1 assuming that the company uses a perpetual inventory system.

Exercise 8-6
Dollar-value LIFO

On January 1, 2003, the Delbridge Company adopted the dollar-value LIFO method for its one inventory pool. The pool's value on this date was $832,000. The 2003 and 2004 ending inventory valued at year-end costs were $954,000 and $975,000, respectively. The appropriate cost indexes are 1.02 for 2003 and 1.05 for 2004.

Required:
Calculate the inventory value at the end of 2003 and 2004 using the dollar-value LIFO method.

PROBLEMS

Problem 8-1
Various inventory transactions; determining inventory and cost of goods sold

The Helmut and King Corporation began 2003 with inventory of 8,000 units of its only product. The units cost $10.00 each. The company uses a periodic inventory system and the LIFO cost method. The following transactions occurred during 2003:

1. Purchased 40,000 additional units at a cost of $11.00 per unit. Terms of the purchases were 2/10, n30, and 80% of the purchases were paid for within the 10 day discount period. The company uses the gross method to record purchase discounts. The merchandise was purchased f.o.b. shipping point and freight charges of $1.00 per unit were paid by Helmut and King.
2. Sales for the year totaled 46,000 units at $20.00 per unit.
3. On December 28, 2003, Helmut and King purchased 5,000 additional units at $12.00 each (price includes freight of $1.00 per unit). The goods were shipped f.o.b. shipping point and arrived at Helmut and King's warehouse on January 4, 2004. The terms of the purchase were n30.
4. 2,000 units were on hand at the end of 2003.

Required:
Determine ending inventory and cost of goods sold for 2003.

Problem 8-2
Various inventory costing methods

Callahan & Sons began 2003 with 10,000 units of its principle product. The cost of each unit is $25.00. Merchandise transactions for the month of January, 2003, are as follows:

Purchases

Date of Purchase	Units	Unit Cost*	Total Cost
Jan. 4	8,000	$ 24.00	$192,000
Jan. 22	7,000	27.00	189,000
Totals	15,000		$381,000

* includes purchase price and cost of freight.

Sales for the month totaled 13,000 units, leaving 12,000 units on hand at the end of the month.

Required:
Calculate January's ending inventory and cost of goods sold for the month using each of the following alternatives:
1. FIFO, periodic system
2. LIFO, periodic system
3. Average cost, periodic system

Exercise 9-1
Lower-of-cost-
or-market

Cooperstown Sports, Inc. has four products in its inventory. Information about the December 31, 2003, inventory is as follows:

Product	Total Cost	Total Replacement Cost	Total Net Realizable Value
Gloves	$360,000	$330,000	$300,000
Bats	260,000	240,000	320,000
Balls	150,000	110,000	125,000
Uniforms	600,000	560,000	950,000

The normal gross profit percentage is 20 percent of *cost*.

Required:
1. Determine the balance sheet inventory carrying value at December 31, 2003, assuming the LCM rule is applied to individual products.
2. Assuming that Cooperstown recognizes an inventory write-down as a separate income statement item, determine the amount of the loss.

Exercise 9-2
Gross profit
method

A fire destroyed a warehouse of the Nicklaus Tire Company on June 17, 2003. Accounting records on that date indicated the following:

Merchandise inventory, January 1, 2003	$ 4,500,000
Purchases to date	14,500,000
Freight-in	1,000,000
Sales to date	23,000,000

The gross profit ratio has averaged 40% of sales for the past three years.

Required:
Use the gross profit method to estimate the cost of the inventory destroyed in the fire.

Exercise 9-3
Retail inventory
method;
average cost

The Alcala Clothing Goods Store uses a periodic inventory system and the retail inventory method to estimate ending inventory and cost of goods sold. The following data is available for the month of May, 2003:

	Cost	Retail
Beginning inventory	$ 40,000	$60,000
Net purchases	28,250	37,000
Net markups		2,000
Net markdowns		1,500
Net sales		45,000

Required:
Estimate the average cost of ending inventory and cost of goods sold for May. Do not approximate LCM.

Alternate Exercises and Problems

Exercise 9-4
Conventional retail method; normal spoilage

The Goodwin Department Store uses the retail inventory method to estimate ending inventory and cost of goods sold. Data for the year 2003 is as follows:

	Cost	Retail
Beginning inventory	$ 180,000	$ 300,000
Purchases	1,479,000	2,430,000
Freight in	30,000	
Purchase returns	60,000	105,000
Net markups		90,000
Net markdowns		45,000
Normal spoilage		63,000
Net sales		2,340,000

Required:
Estimate the ending inventory and cost of goods sold for 2003, applying the conventional retail method (average, LCM).

Exercise 9-5
Dollar-value LIFO retail

On January 1, 2003, the Goldenrod Glass Company adopted the dollar-value LIFO retail method. The following data is available for the year 2003:

	Cost	Retail
Beginning inventory	$213,840	$396,000
Net purchases	360,000	765,000
Net markups		18,000
Net markdowns		33,000
Net sales		690,000
Retail price index, 12/31/03		1.02

Required:
Calculate the estimated ending inventory and cost of goods sold for 2003.

Exercise 9-6
Inventory error

In the year 2003, the internal auditors of Abbott Research, Inc. discovered that goods costing $1.6 million that were shipped f.o.b. shipping point in December of 2002 were in transit on 12/31/02. The goods were recorded as a purchase in December of 2002 but were *not* included in the 2002 year-end inventory.

Required:
Prepare the journal entry needed in 2003 to correct the error. Also, briefly describe any other measures Abbott Research would take in connection with correcting the error. (Ignore income taxes.)

PROBLEMS

Problem 9-1
Retail inventory
method; various
cost methods

Infomania Corporation uses the retail inventory method to estimate ending inventory and cost of goods sold. Data for the year 2003 is as follows:

	Cost	Retail
Beginning inventory	$140,000	$280,000
Purchases	420,000	690,000
Freight in	16,000	
Purchase returns	12,000	18,000
Net markups		24,000
Net markdowns		26,000
Normal spoilage		5,000
Abnormal spoilage		10,000
Sales		700,000
Sales returns		20,000
Employee discounts		6,000

The company records sales net of employee discounts.

Required:
Estimate Infomania's ending inventory and cost of goods sold for the year using the retail inventory method and the following applications:
1. Average cost.
2. Conventional (average, LCM)

Problem 9-2
Dollar-value LIFO
retail method

The Adirondock Company maintains inventory records at selling prices as well as at cost. For the year 2003, the records indicate the following data:

($ in 000s)	Cost	Retail
Beginning inventory	$ 128	$ 200
Purchases	1,072	1,600
Freight-in on purchases	59	
Purchase returns	2	3
Net markups		6
Net markdowns		13
Net sales		1,465

Required:
Assuming the price level increased from 1.00 at January 1 to 1.08 at December 31, 2003, use the dollar-value LIFO retail method to approximate cost of ending inventory and cost of goods sold.

EXERCISES

Exercise 10-1
Goodwill

The Hermanson and Jones Corporation purchased all of the outstanding common stock of Viacon Corporation for $25,000,000 in cash. The book value of Viacon's net assets (assets minus liabilities) was $16,250,000. The fair values of all of Viacon's assets and liabilities were equal to their book values with the following exceptions:

	Book Value	Fair Value
Receivables	$3,000,000	$2,850,000
Property, plant, and equipment	10,200,000	11,200,000
Intangible assets	30,000	3,000,000

Required:
Calculate the amount paid for goodwill.

Exercise 10-2
Acquisition cost; noninterest-bearing note

On January 1, 2003, the Farmington Corporation purchased a packaging and labeling machine. Farmington paid $25,000 down and signed a noninterest-bearing note requiring six annual installments of $10,000 to be paid on each December 31 beginning December 31, 2003. The fair value of the machine is not determinable. An interest rate of 8% properly reflects the time value of money in this situation.

Required:
1. Prepare the journal entry to record the acquisition of the machine. Round computations to the nearest dollar.
2. Prepare the journal entry to record the first payment on December 31, 2003. Round computations to the nearest dollar.
3. Prepare the journal entry to record the second payment on December 31, 2004. Round computations to the nearest dollar.

Exercise 10-3
Nonmonetary exchange; similar assets

The Pioline Company recently traded in a pick-up truck for a newer model truck. The old truck's book value was $1,000 (original cost of $13,000 less $12,000 in accumulated depreciation) and its fair value was $800. Pioline paid $14,000 to complete the exchange.

Required:
Prepare the journal entry to record the exchange.

Exercise 10-4
Nonmonetary exchange; similar assets

[This is a variation of the previous exercise.]

Required:
Assume the same facts as in Exercise 10-3, except that the fair value of the old truck is $1,500. Prepare the journal entry to record the exchange.

Exercise 10-5
Research and
development

The Best and Krieg Company incurred the following research and development costs during 2003:

Salaries and wages for lab research	$ 350,000
Materials used in R&D projects	400,000
Purchase of equipment	85,000
Fees paid to outsiders for R&D projects performed by the outsiders for Best and Krieg	465,000
Patent filing and legal costs for a developed product	20,000
In-process research and development (related to the acquisition of Radon, Inc.)	1,200,000
Total	$2,520,000

The equipment has a 3-year life and has no value beyond the current research project for which it was acquired.

Required:
Calculate the amount of research and development expense that Best and Krieg should report in its 2003 income statement.

Exercise 10-6
Software
development costs

Early in the year 2003, the Adonis Software Company began developing a new software package to be marketed. The software was available for general release to customers in December of 2003. The costs incurred prior to December were $10 million. Of this amount, $6 million was spent before technological feasibility was established. Adonis expects a useful life of three years for the new product with total revenues of $20 million. During 2004, revenue of $5 million was recognized.

Required:
1. Prepare a journal entry to record the 2003 development costs.
2. Calculate the required amortization for 2004.
3. At what amount should the computer software costs be reported in the December 31, 2004 balance sheet?

Intermediate Accounting, 3/e

PROBLEMS

Problem 10-1
Nonmonetary
exchange

On October 15, 2003, the Brown Company exchanged operational assets with the Filzinger Corporation. The facts of the exchange are as follows:

	Brown's Asset	Filzinger's Asset
Original cost	$300,000	$278,000
Accumulated depreciation	200,000	220,000
Fair market value	125,000	110,000

To equalize the exchange, Filzinger paid Brown $15,000 in cash.

Required:
1. Assuming that the assets exchanged are considered *dissimilar* for both companies, record the exchange for both Brown and Filzinger.
2. Assuming that the assets exchanged are considered *similar* for both companies, record the exchange for both Brown and Filzinger.

Problem 10-2
Interest
capitalization;
specific interest
method

On January 1, 2003, the Edinger Manufacturing Company began construction of a building to be used as its office headquarters. The building was completed on June 30, 2004.

Expenditures on the project were as follows:

January 3, 2003	$500,000
March 31, 2003	600,000
June 30, 2003	800,000
October 31, 2003	600,000
January 31, 2004	300,000
March 31, 2004	500,000
May 31, 2004	600,000

On January 3, 2003, the company obtained a $2 million construction loan with a 10% interest rate. The loan was outstanding all of 2003 and 2004. The company's other interest-bearing debt included a long-term note of $5,000,000 with an 8% interest rate, and a mortgage of $3,000,000 on another building with an interest rate of 6%. Both debts were outstanding during all of 2003 and 2004. The company's fiscal year end is December 31.

Required:
1. Calculate the amount of interest that Edinger should capitalize in 2003 and 2004 using the *specific interest method*.
2. What is the total cost of the building?
3. Calculate the amount of interest expense that will appear in the 2003 and 2004 income statements.

Exercise 11-1
Depreciation
methods

On January 1, 2003, the Pattison Corporation purchased machinery for $240,000. The estimated useful life of the machinery is eight years and the estimated residual value is $20,000. The machine is expected to produce 55,000 units during its useful life.

Required:
Calculate depreciation for 2003 and 2004 using each of the following methods. Round all computations to the nearest dollar.
    1. Straight-line.
    2. Sum-of-the-years' digits.
    3. Double-declining balance.
    4. One hundred fifty percent declining balance.
    5. Units-of-production (units produced in 2003, 8,000; units
       produced in 2004, 12,000).

Exercise 11-2
Depreciation
methods; partial
years

[This is a variation of the previous exercise modified to focus on depreciation for partial years.]

On April 30, 2003, the Pattison Corporation purchased machinery for $240,000. The estimated useful life of the machinery is eight years and the estimated residual value is $20,000. The machine is expected to produce 55,000 units during its useful life.

Required:
Calculate depreciation for 2003 and 2004 using each of the following methods. Partial year depreciation is calculated based on the number of months the asset is in service. Round all computations to the nearest dollar.
    1. Straight-line.
    2. Sum-of-the-years' digits.
    3. Double-declining balance.
    4. One hundred fifty percent declining balance.
    5. Units-of-production (units produced in 2003, 6,000; units
       produced in 2004, 12,000).

Exercise 11-3
Depletion

On March 31, 2003, the Allegheny Mining Company purchased the rights to a coal mine. The purchase price plus additional costs necessary to prepare the mine for extraction of the coal totaled $2,000,000. The company expects to extract 1,000,000 tons of coal during a three-year period. During 2003, 400,000 tons were extracted and sold immediately.

Required:
1. Calculate depletion for 2003.
2. Discuss the accounting treatment of the depletion calculated in requirement 1.

Exercise 11-4
Amortization

The Leidecker Company provided the following information on intangible assets:

a. A patent was purchased for $1,000,000 on June 30, 2001. Leidecker estimated the remaining useful life of the patent to be five years.

b. During 2003, a franchise was purchased from the Taco Tio Company for $40,000. The contractual life of the franchise is 20 years and Leidecker records a full year of amortization in the year of purchase.

c. Effective January 1, 2003, based on new events that have occurred, Leidecker estimates that the remaining life of the patent is seven more years.

Required:
1. Prepare the entries necessary to reflect the above information for 2001 through 2003, including year-end adjusting entries to record amortization.
2. Prepare a schedule showing the intangible asset section of the company's December 31, 2003, balance sheet.

Exercise 11-5
Change in estimate; useful life and residual value of equipment

Evergreen Ltd. purchased a cold storage unit on January 2, 2000, at a cost of $640,000. The unit was depreciated using the straight-line method over an estimated 10-year useful life with an estimated residual value of $40,000. On January 1, 2003, the estimate of useful life was changed to a total of 12 years, and the estimate of residual value was changed to $20,000.

Required:
Prepare the appropriate adjusting entry for depreciation in 2003 to reflect the revised estimate.

Exercise 11-6
Error correction

In 2003, the assistant controller of Paddington Industries discovered that in 2000 the company had debited research and development expense for the $200,000 cost of a machine purchased on January 3, 2000. The machine was purchased with the intention that it be used on many different research projects over an expected useful life of eight years. Paddington uses straight-line depreciation and residual value is always set at 10% of cost.

Required:
Prepare the appropriate correcting entry assuming the error was **discovered in 2003** before the adjusting and closing entries. (Ignore income taxes.)

PROBLEMS

Problem 11-1
Partial year
depreciation; asset
addition; increase
in useful life

On May 1, 2001, the Sanderson Electrical Company purchased equipment to be used in its manufacturing process. The equipment cost $60,000, has a six-year useful life and no residual value. The company uses the straight-line depreciation method for all manufacturing equipment.

On January 4, 2003, $15,000 was spent to repair the equipment and to add a feature that increased its operating efficiency. Of the total expenditure, $4,000 represented ordinary repairs and annual maintenance and $11,000 represented the cost of the new feature. In addition to increasing operating efficiency, the total useful life of the equipment was extended to eight years.

Required:
Prepare journal entries for the following:
1. Depreciation for 2001 and 2002.
2. The 2003 expenditure.
3. Depreciation for 2003.

Problem 11-2
Straight-line
depreciation;
change in useful
life and residual
value

The property, plant and equipment section of the Winderl Company's December 31, 2002, balance sheet contained the following:

Property, plant, and equipment:

Land		$410,000
Building	$1,250,000	
Less: accumulated depreciation	300,000	950,000
Equipment	$540,000	
Less: accumulated depreciation	?	?
Total property, plant and equipment		?

The land and building were purchased at the beginning of 1998. Straight-line depreciation is used and a residual value of $50,000 for the building is anticipated. The equipment is comprised of the following three machines:

Machine	Cost	Date Acquired	Residual Value	Life in years
651	$150,000	1/1/00	$10,000	10
652	280,000	6/30/00	- 0 -	7
653	110,000	10/1/02	5,000	8

Early in 2003, the useful life of machine 651 was revised to eight years in total, and the residual value was revised to zero.

Required:
1. Calculate the accumulated depreciation on the equipment at December 31, 2002.
2. Prepare the 2003 year-end adjusting journal entries to record depreciation on the building and equipment.

Problem 11-3
Depreciation and
amortization;
impairment of
operational assets

At the beginning of 2001, Ross Technology, Inc. acquired the Valpo Corporation for $350 million. In addition to cash, receivables, and inventory, the following allocations were made:

Plant and equipment (depreciable assets)	$120 million
Purchased technology	60 million
Goodwill	80 million

The plant and equipment are depreciated over an 8-year useful life on a straight-line basis. There is no estimated residual value. The purchased technology is estimated to have a 6-year useful life, no residual value, and is amortized using the straight-line method.

At the end of 2003, a change in business climate indicated to management that the operational assets of Valpo might be impaired. The following amounts have been determined:

Plant and equipment:
Undiscounted sum of future cash flows	$65 million
Fair value	50 million

Purchased technology:
Undiscounted sum of future cash flows	$15 million
Fair value	10 million

Goodwill:
Fair value of Valpo	$300 million
Fair value of Valpo's net assets (excluding goodwill)	250 million
Book value of Valpo's net assets (including goodwill)	310 million *

*After first recording any impairment losses on plant and equipment and the patent.

Required:
1. Compute the book value of the plant and equipment and purchased technology at the end of 2003.
2. When should the plant and equipment and the purchased technology be tested for impairment?
3. When should goodwill be tested for impairment?
4. Determine the amount of any impairment loss to be recorded, if any, for the three assets

EXERCISES

Exercise 12-1
Various transactions related to securities available for sale

Parnell Industries buys securities to be available for sale when circumstances warrant, *not* to profit from short-term differences in price and *not* necessarily to hold debt securities to maturity. The following selected transactions relate to investment activities of Parnell Industries whose fiscal year ends on December 31. No investments were held by Parnell at the beginning of the year.

2003

March 1	Purchased 2 million Platinum Gems, Inc. common shares for $124 million, including brokerage fees and commissions.
April 13	Purchased $200 million of 10% bonds at face value from Oracle Wholesale Corporation.
July 20	Received cash dividends of $3 million on the investment in Platinum Gems, Inc. common shares.
October 13	Received semiannual interest of $10 million on the investment in Oracle bonds.
October 14	Sold the Oracle bonds for $205 million.
November 1	Purchased 500,000 SPI International preferred shares for $40 million, including brokerage fees and commissions.
December 31	Recorded the necessary adjusting entry(s) relating to the investments. The market prices of the investments are $64 per share for Platinum Gems, Inc. and $74 per share for SPI International preferred shares.

2004

January 25	Sold half the Platinum Gems, Inc. shares for $65 per share.
March 1	Sold the SPI International preferred shares for $78 per share.

Required:
1. Prepare the appropriate journal entry for each transaction or event.
2. Show the amounts that would be reported on the company's 2003 income statement relative to these investments.

Exercise 12-2
Various investment securities

At December 31, 2003, McKnight Brothers Corp. had the following investments that were purchased during 2000, its first year of operations:

	Cost	Fair Value
Trading Securities:		
Security A	$ 700,000	$ 725,000
B	210,000	200,000
Totals	$ 910,000	$ 925,000
Securities Available for Sale:		
Security C	$ 500,000	$ 560,000
D	850,000	865,000
Totals	$1,350,000	$1,425,000
Securities to Be Held to Maturity:		
Security E	$ 970,000	$ 980,000
F	412,000	409,000
Totals	$1,382,000	$1,389,000

No investments were sold during 2003. All securities except Security D and Security F are considered short-term investments. None of the market changes is considered permanent.

Required:
Determine the following amounts at December 31, 2003:
1. Investments reported as current assets.
2. Investments reported as noncurrent assets.
3. Unrealized gain (or loss) component of income before taxes.
4. Unrealized gain (or loss) component of shareholders' equity.

Exercise 12-3
Equity method; purchase; investee income; dividends

As a long-term investment at the beginning of the fiscal year, Paper Products International purchased 35% of Reed's Restaurant Supplies, Inc.'s 12 million shares for $73 million. The fair value and book value of the shares were the same at that time. During the year, Reed's Restaurant Supplies earned net income of $20 million and distributed cash dividends of $1.10 per share. At the end of the year, the fair value of the shares is $59 million.

Required:
Prepare the appropriate journal entries from the purchase through the end of the year.

Exercise 12-4
Equity method;
adjustments for
depreciation

J & W Leasing paid $76 million on January 4, 2003, for 5 million shares of Conley Trucks common stock. The investment represents a 25% interest in the net assets of Conley and gave J & W the ability to exercise significant influence over Conley's operations. J & W received dividends of $1.20 per share on December 27, 2003, and Conley reported net income of $60 million for the year ended December 31, 2003. The market value of Conley's common stock at December 31, 2003, was $22.25 per share.

- The book value of Conley's net assets was $212 million.
- The fair market value of Conley's depreciable assets exceeded their book value by $40 million. These assets had an average remaining useful life of 5 years.
- The remainder of the excess of the cost of the investment over the book value of net assets purchased was attributable to goodwill.

Required:
Prepare all appropriate journal entries related to the investment during 2003.

PROBLEMS

Problem 12-1
Investment
securities and
equity method
investments
compared

On January 4, 2003, RTN Industries paid $648,000 for 20,000 shares of Austin Cattle Company common stock. The investment represents a 30% interest in the net assets of Austin and gave RTN the ability to exercise significant influence over Austin's operations. RTN received dividends of $3.00 per share on December 6, 2003, and Austin reported net income of $320,000 for the year ended December 31, 2003. The market value of Austin's common stock at December 31, 2003, was $32 per share. The book value of Austin's net assets was $1,600,000 and:

a. The fair market value of Austin's depreciable assets, with an average remaining useful life of 8 years, exceeded their book value by $160,000.
b. The remainder of the excess of the cost of the investment over the book value of net assets purchased was attributable to goodwill.

Required:
1. Prepare all appropriate journal entries related to the investment during 2003, assuming RTN accounts for this investment by the equity method.
2. Prepare the journal entries required by RTN, assuming that the 20,000 shares represents a 10% interest in the net assets of Austin rather than a 30% interest.

Problem 12-2
Equity method

Southeast Pulp and Paper, a paper and allied products manufacturer, was seeking to gain a foothold in Mexico. Toward that end, the company bought 40% of the outstanding common shares of Monterrey Milling, Inc. on January 3, 2003, for $80 million.

At the date of purchase, the book value of Monterrey's net assets was $155 million. The book values and fair values for all balance sheet items were the same except for inventory and plant facilities. The fair value exceeded book value by $1 million for the inventory and by $4 million for the plant facilities.

The estimated useful life of the plant facilities is 8 years. All inventory acquired was sold during 2003.

Monterrey reported net income of $28 million for the year ended December 31, 2000. Monterrey paid a cash dividend of $6 million.

Required:
1. Prepare all appropriate journal entries related to the investment during 2003.
2. What amount should Southeast report as its income from its investment in Monterrey for the year ended December 31, 2003?
3. What amount should Southeast report on its balance sheet as its investment in Monterrey?
4. What should Southeast report on its statement of cash flows regarding its investment in Monterrey?

EXERCISES

Exercise 13-1
Bank loan; accrued interest

On September 1, 2003, Tri-State Paving Inc., an asphalt resurfacing and repairing company, borrowed $6 million cash to fund a twenty mile highway project. The loan was made by Alabama TrustCorp under a noncommitted short-term line of credit arrangement. Tri-State issued a 6-month, 14% promissory note. Interest was payable at maturity. Tri-State's fiscal period is the calendar year.

Required:
1. Prepare the journal entry for the issuance of the note by Tri-State Paving Inc.
2. Prepare the appropriate adjusting entry for the note by Tri-State on December 31, 2003.
3. Prepare the journal entry for the payment of the note at maturity.

Exercise 13-2
Determining accrued interest in various situations

On May 1, 2003, Ex-Cel Industries issued 9-month notes in the amount of $300 million. Interest is payable at maturity.

Required:
Determine the amount of interest expense that should be recorded in a year-end adjusting entry under each of the following independent assumptions:

	Interest rate	Fiscal Year End
1.	13%	December 31
2.	10%	October 31
3.	9%	June 30
4.	7%	January 31

Exercise 13-3
Short-term notes

The following selected transactions relate to liabilities of Odyssey Travel Corporation. Odyssey's fiscal year ends on December 31.

Required:
Prepare the appropriate journal entries through the maturity of each liability.

2003

Jan. 22   Negotiated a revolving credit agreement with Massey Bank which can be renewed annually upon bank approval. The amount available under the line of credit is $6,000,000 at the bank's prime rate.

Mar. 1   Arranged a 3-month bank loan of $7 million with Massey Bank under the line of credit agreement. Interest at the prime rate of 10% was payable at maturity.

June 1   Paid the 10% note at maturity.

Nov. 1   Supported by the credit line, issued $6 million of commercial paper on a nine-month note. Interest was discounted at issuance at a 8% discount rate.

Dec. 31   Recorded any necessary adjusting entry(s).

2004

Aug. 1   Paid the commercial paper at maturity.

Exercise 13-4
Current –
noncurrent
classification of
debt

At December 31, 2003, Parker Petroleum's liabilities include the following:

1. $22 million of 10% notes are due on March 31, 2008. A debt covenant requires Parker to maintain current assets at least equal to 150% of its current liabilities. On December 31, 2003, Parker is in violation of this covenant. Parker obtained a waiver from City Corp Bank until June 2004, having convinced the bank that the company's normal 2 to 1 ratio of current assets to current liabilities will be reestablished during the first half of 2004.

2. $9 million of noncallable 13% bonds were issued for $9 million on September 30, 1972. The bonds mature on August 31, 2004. Sufficient cash is expected to be available to retire the bonds at maturity.

3. $15 million of 10% bonds were issued for $15 million on June 30, 1983. The bonds mature on June 30, 2013, but bondholders have the option of calling (demanding payment on) the bonds on June 30, 2004. However, the call option is not expected to be exercised, given prevailing market conditions.

Required:
What portion of the debt can be excluded from classification as a current liability (that is, reported as a noncurrent liability)? Explain.

Exercise 13-5
Warranties

Safe-Loc Security Door Corp. introduced a new line of commercial security doors in 2003 that carry a four-year warranty against manufacturer's defects. Based on their experience with previous product introductions, warranty costs are expected to approximate 4% of sales. Sales and actual warranty expenditures for the first year of selling the product were:

Sales	Actual warranty expenditures
$7,500,000	$124,800

Required:

1. Does this situation represent a loss contingency? Why or why not? How should it be accounted for?

2. Prepare journal entries that summarize sales of the security doors (assume all credit sales) and any aspects of the warranty that should be recorded during 2003.

3. What amount should Safe-Loc report as a liability at December 31, 2003?

PROBLEMS

Problem 13-1
Bank loan: accrued interest

Schilling Motors, borrowed $42 million cash on November 1, 2003, to provide working capital for year-end inventory. Schilling issued a 5-month, 12% promissory note to First Bank under a prearranged short-term line of credit. Interest on the note was payable at maturity. Each firm's fiscal period is the calendar year.

Required:
1. Prepare the journal entries to record (a) the issuance of the note by Schilling and (b) First Bank's receivable on November 1, 2003.
2. Prepare the journal entries by both firms to record all subsequent events related to the note through March 31, 2004.
3. Suppose the face amount of the note was adjusted to include interest (a noninterest-bearing note) and 12% is the bank's stated "discount rate." Prepare the journal entries to record the issuance of the noninterest-bearing note by Schilling on November 1, 2003. What would be the effective interest rate?

Problem 13-2
Various contingencies

Finley Roofing is involved with several situations that possibly involve contingencies. Each is described below. Finley's fiscal year ends December 31, and the 2003 financial statements are issued on March 20, 2004.
1. Finley is involved in a lawsuit resulting from a dispute with a customer. On January 25, 2004, judgment was rendered against Finley in the amount of $34 million plus interest, a total of $36 million. Finley plans to appeal the judgment and is unable to predict its outcome though it is not expected to have a material adverse effect on the company.
2. At March 20, 2004, the IRS is in the process of auditing Finley's tax returns for 2001-2003, but has not proposed a deficiency assessment. Management feels an assessment is reasonably possible, and if an assessment is made an unfavorable settlement of up to $15 million is reasonably possible.
3. Finley is the plaintiff in a $80 million lawsuit filed against AA Asphalt for damages due to lost profits from rejected contracts and for unpaid receivables. The case is in final appeal and legal counsel advises that it is probable that Finley will prevail and be awarded $75 million.
4. In October 2002, the State of Montana filed suit against Finley, seeking civil penalties and injunctive relief for violations of environmental laws regulating hazardous waste. On February 3, 2004, Finley reached a settlement with state authorities. Based upon discussions with legal counsel, the Company feels it is probable that $55 million will be required to cover the cost of violations. Eastern believes that the ultimate settlement of this claim will not have a material adverse effect on the company.

Required:
1. Determine the appropriate means of reporting each situation. Explain your reasoning.
2. Prepare any necessary journal entries and disclosure notes.

EXERCISES

Exercise 14-1
Accrued interest

On March 1, 2003, CMT Corporation issued $50 million of 12% bonds, dated January 1, 2003, for $47 million (plus accrued interest). The bonds mature on December 31, 2021, and pay interest semiannually on June 30 and December 31. CMT's fiscal period is the calendar year.

Required:
1. Determine the amount of accrued interest that was included in the proceeds received from the bond sale.
2. Prepare the journal entry for the issuance of the bonds by CMT.

Exercise 14-2
Determine the price of bonds; issuance; effective interest; no amortization schedule

Ticket, Inc. issued 10% bonds, dated January 1, with a face amount of $240 million on January 1, 2003. The bonds mature in 2013 (10 years). For bonds of similar risk and maturity the market yield is 12%. Interest is paid semiannually on June 30 and December 31.

Required:
1. Determine the price of the bonds at January 1, 2003.
2. Prepare the journal entry to record their issuance by Ticket on January 1, 2003.
3. Prepare the journal entry to record interest on June 30, 2003 (at the effective rate). [Do not prepare an amortization schedule.]
4. Prepare the journal entry to record interest on December 31, 2003 (at the effective rate). [Do not prepare an amortization schedule.]

Exercise 14-3
Convertible bonds

On January 1, 2003, Schmidt Security issued $60 million of 9%, 10-year convertible bonds at 102. The bonds pay interest on June 30 and December 31. Each $1,000 bond is convertible into 40 shares of Schmidt's $1 par common stock. Facial Mapping Company purchased 10% of the issue as an investment.

Required:
1. Prepare the journal entries for the issuance of the bonds by Schmidt and the purchase of the bond investment by Facial Mapping.
2. Prepare the journal entries for the June 30, 2007, interest payment by both Schmidt and Facial Mapping assuming both use the straight-line method.
3. On July 1, 2008, when Schmidt's common stock had a market price of $33 per share, Facial Mapping converted the bonds it held. Prepare the journal entries by both Schmidt and Facial Mapping for the conversion of the bonds (book value method).

PROBLEMS

Problem 14-1
Straight-line and effective interest compared

On January 1, 2003, Lamb Services issued $200,000, 9%, four-year bonds. Interest is paid semiannually on June 30 and December 31. The bonds were issued at $193,537 to yield an annual return of 10%.

Required:
1. Prepare an amortization schedule that determines interest at the effective interest rate.
2. Prepare an amortization schedule by the straight-line method.
3. Prepare the journal entries to record interest expense on June 30, 2005, by each of the two approaches.
4. Explain why the pattern of interest differs between the two methods.
5. Assuming the market rate is still 10%, what price would a second investor pay the first investor on June 30, 2005, for $20,000 of the bonds?

Problem 14-2
Note and installment note with unrealistic interest rate

Warren Machinery, Inc. constructed an industrial lathe for Nelson Equipment that was completed and ready for use on January 1, 2003. Nelson paid for the conveyor by issuing a $500,000, 4-year note that specified 5% interest to be paid on December 31 of each year. The conveyor was custom-built for Nelson so its cash price was unknown. By comparison with similar transactions it was determined that a reasonable interest rate was 10%.

Required:
1. Prepare the journal entry for Nelson's purchase of the conveyor on January 1, 2003.
2. Prepare an amortization schedule for the four-year term of the note.
3. Prepare the journal entry for Nelson's third interest payment on December 31, 2005.
4. If Nelson's note had been an installment note to be paid in four equal payments at the end of each year beginning December 31, 2003, what would be the amount of each installment?
5. Prepare an amortization schedule for the four-year term of the installment note.
6. Prepare the journal entry for Nelson's third installment payment on December 31, 2005.

Problem 14-3
Accrued interest;
effective interest;
financial statement
effects

On February 28, 2003, Pujols Industries issued 10% bonds, dated January 1, with a face amount of $48 million. The bonds were priced at $42 million (plus accrued interest) to yield is 12%. Interest is paid semiannually on June 30 and December 31. Pujols' fiscal year ends September 30.

Required:
1. What would be the amount(s) related to the bonds Pujols would report in its balance sheet at October 31, 2003?
2. What would be the amount(s) related to the bonds that Pujols would report in its income statement for the year ended October 31, 2003?
3. What would be the amount(s) related to the bonds that Pujols would report in its statement of cash flows for the year ended October 31, 2003?

Problem 14-4
Early
extinguishment

The long-term liability section of Westin Laboratories balance sheet as of December 31, 2002, included 10% bonds having a face amount of $200 million and a remaining premium of $30 million. On January 1, 2003, Eastern Post retired some of the bonds before their scheduled maturity.

Required:
Prepare the journal entry by Westin to record the redemption of the bonds under each of the independent circumstances below:
1. Westin called half the bonds at the call price of 102 (102% of face amount).
2. Westin repurchased $50 million of the bonds on the open market at their market price of $52.5 million.

EXERCISES

Exercise 15-1
Operating Lease

On January 1, 2003, Gothic Corporation, an internet training firm, leased several computers from HardWhere Inc. under a 3-year operating lease agreement. The contract calls for four rent payments of $40,000 each, payable semiannually on June 30 and December 31 each year. The computers were acquired by HardWhere at a cost of $350,000 and were expected to have a useful life of 5 years with no residual value.

Required:
Prepare the appropriate entries for both (a) the lessee and (b) the lessor from the inception of the lease through the end of 2003. (Use straight-line depreciation.)

Exercise 15-2
Capital lease; lessee

[Note: Exercises 2, 3, and 4 are three variations of the same basic situation.]
Manufacturers Eastern leased high-tech electronic equipment from Franklin Leasing on January 1, 2003. Franklin purchased the equipment from National Machines at a cost of $107,866.

Related information:

Lease term	3 years (12 quarterly periods)
Quarterly rental payments	$10,000 - beginning of each period
Economic life of asset	3 years
Fair value of asset	$107,866
Implicit interest rate	8%
(Also lessee's incremental borrowing rate)	

Required:
Prepare a lease amortization schedule and appropriate entries for Manufacturers Eastern from the inception of the lease through January 1, 2004. Depreciation is recorded at the end of each fiscal year (December 31) on a straight-line basis.

Exercise 15-3
Direct financing lease; lessor

[Note: Exercises 2, 3, and 4 are three variations of the same basic situation.]
Franklin Leasing leased high-tech electronic equipment to Manufacturers Eastern on January 1, 2003. Franklin purchased the equipment from National Machines at a cost of $107,866.

Related information:

Lease term	3 years (12 quarterly periods)
Quarterly rental payments	$10,000 - beginning of each period
Economic life of asset	3 years
Fair value of asset	$107,866
Implicit interest rate	8%
(Also lessee's incremental borrowing rate)	

Required:
Prepare a lease amortization schedule and appropriate entries for Franklin Leasing from the inception of the lease through January 1, 2004. Franklin's fiscal year ends December 31.

Exercise 15-4

Sales-type lease; lessor

[Note: Exercises 2, 3, and 4 are three variations of the same basic situation.]

Manufacturers Eastern leased high-tech electronic equipment from National Machines on January 1, 2003. National Machines manufactured the equipment at a cost of $90,000.

Related information:

Lease term	3 years (12 quarterly periods)
Quarterly rental payments	$10,000 - beginning of each period
Economic life of asset	3 years
Fair value of asset	$107,866
Implicit interest rate	8%

   (Also lessee's incremental borrowing rate)

Required:

1. Show how National Machines determined the $10,000 quarterly rental payments.
2. Prepare appropriate entries for National Machines to record the lease at its inception, January 1, 2000, and the second rental payment on April 1, 2003.

Exercise 15-5

Sale-leaseback; capital lease

To raise operating funds, WSMM Broadcasting sold a helicopter used in news reports on January 1, 2003, to a finance company for $1,540,000. WSMM immediately leased the helicopter back for a 13-year period, at which time ownership of the helicopter will transfer to WSMM. The helicopter has a fair value of $1,600,000. Its cost and its carrying value were $1,240,000. Its useful life is estimated to be 20 years. The lease requires WSMM to make payments of $205,542 to the finance company each January 1. WSMM depreciates assets on a straight-line basis. The lease has an implicit rate of 11%.

Required:

Prepare the appropriate entries for WSMM on (a) January 1, 2003, to record the sale-leaseback and (b) December 31, 2003, to record necessary adjustments.

Problem 15-1
Direct financing and sales-type lease; lessee and lessor

Tech-Knowledgies develops and manufactures voice recognition hardware. Star Leasing purchased a voice recognition hardware from Tech-Knowledgies for $500,000 and leased it to Pal Learning Systems on January 1, 2003.

Lease description:

Quarterly rental payments	$32,629 - beginning of each period
Lease term	5 years (20 quarters)
No residual value; no BPO	
Economic life of lithotripter	5 years
Implicit interest rate and lessee's incremental borrowing rate	12%
Fair value of asset	$500,000

Collectibility of the rental payments is reasonably assured, and there are no lessor costs yet to be incurred.

Required:

1. How should this lease be classified by Pal Learning Systems and by Star Leasing?
2. Prepare appropriate entries for both Pal Learning Systems and Star Leasing from the inception of the lease through the second rental payment on April 1, 2003. Depreciation is recorded at the end of each fiscal year (December 31).
3. Assume Pal Learning Systems leased the hardware directly from the manufacturer, Tech-Knowledgies, which produced the machine at a cost of $450,000. Prepare appropriate entries for Tech-Knowledgies from the inception of the lease through the second rental payment on April 1, 2003.

Problem 15-2
Guaranteed
residual value;
direct financing
lease

On December 31, 2003, HHH Corp. leased equipment to Blair Co. for a 4-year period ending December 31, 2007, at which time possession of the leased asset will revert back to HHH Corp. The equipment cost HHH Corp. $1,097,280 and has an expected useful life of 6 years. Its normal sales price is $1,097,280. The lessee-guaranteed residual value at December 31, 2008, is $75,000. Equal payments under the lease are $300,000 and are due on December 31 of each year. The first payment was made on December 31, 2003. Collectibility of the remaining lease payments is reasonably assured, and HHH Corp. has no material cost uncertainties. Blair's incremental borrowing rate is 12%. Blair knows the interest rate implicit in the lease payments is 10%. Both companies use straight-line depreciation.

Required:
1. Show how HHH Corp. calculated the $300,000 annual rental payments.
2. How should this lease be classified (a) by Blair Co. (the lessee) and (b) by HHH Corp. (the lessor)? Why?
3. Prepare the appropriate entries for both Blair Co. and HHH Corp. on December 31, 2003.
4. Prepare an amortization schedule(s) that describes the pattern of interest over the lease term for the lessee and the lessor.
5. Prepare all appropriate entries for both Blair and HHH Corp. on December 31, 2004 (the second rent payment and depreciation).
6. Prepare the appropriate entries for both Blair and HHH Corp. on December 31, 2007 (the end of the lease), assuming the equipment is returned to HHH Corp. and the actual residual value on that date is $4,500.

EXERCISES

Exercise 16-1
Single temporary difference; taxable income given

Stancil Industries reports *pretax accounting income* of $80 million, but due to a single temporary difference, *taxable income* is only $50 million. At the beginning of the year, no temporary differences existed.

Required:
Assuming a tax rate of 35%, prepare the appropriate journal entry to record Stancil's income taxes.

Exercise 16-2
Single temporary difference; income tax payable given

In 2003, Lambert Services collected rent revenue for 2004 tenant occupancy. For income tax reporting, the rent is taxed when collected. For financial statement reporting, the rent is recognized as income in the period earned. The unearned portion of the rent collected in 2003 amounted to $90,000 at December 31, 2003. Lambert had no temporary differences at the beginning of the year.

Required:
Assuming an income tax rate of 40%, and that the 2003 income tax payable is $285,000, prepare the journal entry to record income taxes for 2003.

Exercise 16-3
Deferred tax asset; income tax payable given; previous balance in valuation allowance

At the end of 2002, Mathis Industries had a deferred tax asset account with a balance of $120 million attributable to a temporary book-tax difference of $300 million in a liability for estimated expenses. At the end of 2003, the temporary difference is $280 million. Mathis has no other temporary differences. Taxable income for 2003 is $720 million and the tax rate is 40%.

Mathis has a valuation allowance of $40 million for the deferred tax asset at the beginning of 2003.

Required:
1. Prepare the journal entry(s) to record Mathis's income taxes for 2003 assuming it is "more likely than not" that the deferred tax asset will be realized.
2. Prepare the journal entry(s) to record Mathis's income taxes for 2003 assuming it is "more likely than not" that one-half of the deferred tax asset will not ultimately be realized.

Exercise 16-4
Single temporary
difference; non-
temporary
difference;
calculate taxable
income

Fessler Transport began operations in January 2003, and purchased a delivery truck for $160,000.

Fessler plans to use straight-line depreciation over a four-year expected useful life for financial reporting purposes. For tax purposes, the deduction is 50% of cost in 2003, 30% in 2004, and 20% in 2005. Pretax accounting income for 2003 was $900,000, which includes interest revenue of $160,000 from municipal bonds. The enacted tax rate is 40%.

Required:

Assuming no differences between accounting income and taxable income other than those described above:
1. Prepare the journal entry to record income taxes in 2003.
2. What is Fessler's 2003 net income?

The following income statement does not reflect intraperiod tax allocation.

Income Statement
For the fiscal year ended June 30, 2003

	($ in millions)
Revenues	$415
Cost of goods sold	(175)
Gross profit	$240
Operating expenses	(90)
Income tax expense	(42)
Income before extraordinary item and cumulative effect of accounting change	$108
Extraordinary casualty loss	(5)
Cumulative effect of change in depreciation methods	(40)
Net income	$ 63

The company's tax rate is 40%.

Required:

Recast the income statement to reflect intraperiod tax allocation.

Problem 16-1
Change in tax rate;
single temporary
difference

Commercial Development began operations in December 2003. When lots for industrial development are sold, Commercial recognizes income for financial reporting purposes in the year of the sale. For some lots, Commercial recognizes income for tax purposes when collected. Income recognized for financial reporting purposes in 2003 for lots sold this way was $48 million which will be collected over the next three years. Scheduled collections for 2004-2006 are as follows:

2004	$ 16 million
2005	20 million
2006	12 million
	$48 million

Pretax *accounting* income for 2003 was $68 million. The enacted tax rate is 40 percent.

Required:
1. Assuming no differences between accounting income and taxable income other than those described above, prepare the journal entry to record income taxes in 2003.
2. Suppose a new tax law, revising the tax rate from 40% to 35%, beginning in 2004, is *enacted in 2004*, when pretax accounting income was $60 million. Prepare the appropriate journal entry to record income taxes in 2004.
3. If the new tax rate had not been enacted, what would have been the appropriate balance in the deferred tax liability account at the end of 2004? Why?

Problem 16-2
Operating loss
carryback and
carryforward;
temporary
difference; non-
temporary
difference

CPS Corporation reported a pretax operating loss of $540,000 for financial reporting purposes in 2003. Contributing to the loss were (a) a penalty of $20,000 assessed by the Environmental Protection Agency for violation of a federal law and paid in 2003 and (b) an estimated loss of $40,000 from accruing a loss contingency. The loss will be tax deductible when paid in 2004.

The enacted tax rate is 40%. There were no temporary differences at the beginning of the year and none originating in 2003 other than those described above. Taxable income in CPS's two previous years of operation was as follows:

2001	300,000
2002	120,000

Required:

1. Prepare the journal entry to recognize the income tax benefit of the operating loss in 2003. CPS elects the carryback option.
2. Show the lower portion of the 2003 income statement that reports the income tax benefit of the operating loss.
3. Prepare the journal entry to record income taxes in 2004 assuming pretax accounting income is $240,000. No additional temporary differences originate in 2004.

EXERCISES

Exercise 17-1
Determine pension expense

Hunt Industries has a noncontributory, defined benefit pension plan. At December 31, 2003, Hunt received the following information:

Projected Benefit obligation	($ in millions)
Balance, January 1	$360
Service cost	60
Interest cost	36
Benefits paid	(27)
Balance, December 31	$429

Plan Assets	
Balance, January 1	$240
Actual return on plan assets	27
Contributions 2003	60
Benefits paid	(27)
Balance, December 31	$300

The expected long-term rate of return on plan assets was 10%. There was no unrecognized prior service cost, gains and losses, or transition cost on January 1, 2003.

Required:
1. Determine Hunt's pension expense for 2003.
2. Prepare the journal entry to record Hunt's pension expense and funding for 2003.

Exercise 17-2
Minimum liability

C&D Consulting has a defined benefit pension plan. C&D's policy is to fund the plan annually, cash payments being made at the end of each year. Data relating to the pension plan for 2003 are as follows:

	($ in millions)
Prepaid (accrued) pension cost at the beginning of the year – debit balance	$ 40
Net pension expense for 2003	200
Unrecognized prior service cost at year end	150
Accumulated benefit obligation at year end	585
Projected benefit obligation at year end	700
Fair value of plan assets at year end	520
Payment to trustee at year end	190

Required:
Determine C&D's pension liability to be reported on the 2003 balance sheet and prepare any journal entry necessary to achieve that reporting objective.

PROBLEMS

Problem 17-1
ABO calculations; present value concepts

[Problems 1 – 5 are variations of the same situation, designed to focus on different elements of the pension plan.]

D&C Advisory's defined benefit pension plan specifies annual retirement benefits equal to: 1.5% x service years x final year's salary, payable at the end of each year. Bobby Flay was hired by D&C at the beginning of 1989 and is expected to retire at the end of 2033 after 45 years service. His retirement is expected to span 18 years. Flay's salary is $80,000 at the end of 2003, and the company's actuary projects his salary to be $250,000 at retirement. The actuary's discount rate is 7%.

Required:
1. Draw a time line that depicts Flay's expected service period, retirement period, and a 2003 measurement date for the pension obligation.
2. Estimate by the accumulated benefits approach the amount of Flay's annual retirement payments earned as of the end of 2003.
3. What is the company's accumulated benefit obligation at the end of 2003 with respect to Flay?
4. If no estimates are changed in the meantime, what will be the accumulated benefit obligation at the end of 2005 (two years later) when Flay's salary is $85,000?

Problem 17-2
PBO calculations; present value concepts

[Problems 1 – 5 are variations of the same situation, designed to focus on different elements of the pension plan.]

D&C Advisory's defined benefit pension plan specifies annual retirement benefits equal to: 1.5% x service years x final year's salary, payable at the end of each year. Bobby Flay was hired by D&C at the beginning of 1989 and is expected to retire at the end of 2033 after 45 years service. His retirement is expected to span 18 years. Flay's salary is $80,000 at the end of 2003, and the company's actuary projects his salary to be $250,000 at retirement. The actuary's discount rate is 7%.

Required:
1. Draw a time line that depicts Flay's expected service period, retirement period, and a 2003 measurement date for the pension obligation.
2. Estimate by the projected benefits approach the amount of Flay's annual retirement payments earned as of the end of 2003.
3. What is the company's projected benefit obligation at the end of 2003 with respect to Flay?
4. If no estimates are changed in the meantime, what will be the projected benefit obligation at the end of 2005 (two years later) when Flay's salary is $85,000?

Problem 17-3
Service cost, interest, and PBO calculations; present value concepts

[Problems 1 – 5 are variations of the same situation, designed to focus on different elements of the pension plan.]

D&C Advisory's defined benefit pension plan specifies annual retirement benefits equal to: 1.5% x service years x final year's salary, payable at the end of each year. Bobby Flay was hired by D&C at the beginning of 1989 and is expected to retire at the end of 2033 after 45 years service. His retirement is expected to span 18 years. Flay's salary is $80,000 at the end of 2003, and the company's actuary projects his salary to be $250,000 at retirement. The actuary's discount rate is 7%.

Required:
1. What is the company's projected benefit obligation at the *beginning* of 2003 (after 14 years' service) with respect to Flay?
2. Estimate by the projected benefits approach the portion of Flay's annual retirement payments attributable to 2003 service.
3. What is the company's service cost for 2003 with respect to Flay?
4. What is the company's interest cost for 2003 with respect to Flay?
5. Combine your answers to requirements 1, 3, and 4 to determine the company's projected benefit obligation at the *end* of 2003 (after 15 years' service) with respect to Flay?

Problem 17-4
Prior service cost; components of pension expense; present value concepts

[Problems 1 – 5 are variations of the same situation, designed to focus on different elements of the pension plan.]

D&C Advisory's defined benefit pension plan specifies annual retirement benefits equal to: 1.5% x service years x final year's salary, payable at the end of each year. Bobby Flay was hired by D&C at the beginning of 1989 and is expected to retire at the end of 2033 after 45 years service. His retirement is expected to span 18 years. Flay's salary is $80,000 at the end of 2003, and the company's actuary projects his salary to be $250,000 at retirement. The actuary's discount rate is 7%.

At the beginning of 2001, the pension formula was amended to:

    1.65% x service years x final year's salary

The amendment was made retroactive to apply the increased benefits to prior service years.

Required:
1. What is the company's prior service cost at the beginning of 2004 with respect to Flay after the amendment described above?
2. Since the amendment occurred at the *beginning* of 2004, amortization of the prior service cost begins in 2004. What is the prior service cost amortization that would be included in pension expense?
3. What is the service cost for 2004 with respect to Flay?
4. What is the interest cost for 2004 with respect to Flay?
5. Calculate pension expense for 2004 with respect to Flay assuming plan assets attributable to him of $170,000 and a rate of return (actual and expected) of 10%.

[Problems 1 – 5 are variations of the same situation, designed to focus on different elements of the pension plan.]

D&C Advisory's defined benefit pension plan specifies annual retirement benefits equal to: 1.5% x service years x final year's salary, payable at the end of each year. Bobby Flay was hired by D&C at the beginning of 1989 and is expected to retire at the end of 2033 after 45 years service. His retirement is expected to span 18 years. Flay's salary is $80,000 at the end of 2003, and the company's actuary projects his salary to be $250,000 at retirement. The actuary's discount rate is 7%.

At the beginning of 2004, changing economic conditions caused the actuary to reassess the applicable discount rate. It was decided that 6% is the appropriate rate.

Required:
Calculate the effect of the change in the assumed discount rate on the PBO at the beginning of 2004 with respect to Flay.

EXERCISES

Exercise 18-1
Postretirement
benefits;
determine the
APBO and
service cost

Love Industries has an unfunded postretirement health care benefit plan. Medical care benefits are provided to employees who render 10 years service and attain age 57 while in service. At the end of 2003, Larry Abbott is 31. He was hired by Love at age 27 (6 years ago) and is expected to retire at age 64. The expected postretirement benefit obligation for Abbott at the end of 2003 is $200,000 and $216,000 at the end of 2004.

Required:
Calculate the *accumulated postretirement benefit obligation* at the end of 2003 and 2004 and the *service cost* for 2003 and 2004 as pertaining to Abbott.

Exercise 18-2
Postretirement
benefits;
amortization of
unrecognized
transition
obligation and
prior service cost

Tomorrow, Inc. provides postretirement health care benefits to employees who provide at least 14 years service and reach age 61 while in service. On January 1, 2003, the following plan-related data were available:

	($ in millions)
Unrecognized transition obligation	$ 100
Accumulated postretirement benefit obligation	210
Fair value of plan assets	none
Average remaining service period to retirement	20 years
Average remaining service period to full eligibility	15 years

On January 1, 2003, Tomorrow amends the plan to provide certain dental benefits in addition to previously provided medical benefits. The actuary determines that the cost of making the amendment retroactive increases the APBO by $30 million. Management chooses to amortize the prior service cost on a straight-line basis. The service cost for 2003 is $61 million. The interest rate is 5%.

Required:
Calculate the postretirement benefit expense for 2003.

Exercise 18-3
Restricted stock award plan; forfeitures anticipated

LaRue Industries offers a variety of stock-based compensation plans to employees. Under its restricted stock award plan, the company on January 1, 2003, granted 12 million of its $1 par common shares to various regional managers. The shares are subject to forfeiture if employment is terminated within 3 years. The common shares have a market price of $25.50 per share on the grant date.

Required:
1. Determine the total compensation cost pertaining to the restricted shares.
2. Prepare the appropriate journal entry to record the award of restricted shares on January 1, 2003.
3. Prepare the appropriate journal entry to record compensation expense on December 31, 2003.
4. Suppose LaRue expected a 20% forfeiture rate on the restricted shares prior to vesting. Determine the total compensation cost, assuming the company chooses to follow the elective fair value approach for fixed compensation plans and chooses to anticipate forfeitures at the grant date.

Exercise 18-4
Stock option plan; elective fair value approach; forfeiture of options

On January 1, 2003, MEM Corporation granted 75,000 incentive stock options to branch managers, each permitting holders to purchase one share of the company's $1 par common shares within the next 7 years, but not before December 31, 2007 (the vesting date). The exercise price is the market price of the shares on the date of grant, currently $20 per share. The fair value of the options, estimated by an appropriate option pricing model, is $7 per option. MEM chooses to follow the elective fair value approach for fixed compensation plans.

Required:
1. Determine the total compensation cost pertaining to the options on January 1, 2003.
2. Prepare the appropriate journal entry to record compensation expense on December 31, 2003.
3. Unexpected turnover during 2004 caused the forfeiture of 10% of the stock options. Determine the adjusted compensation cost, and prepare the appropriate journal entry(s) on December 31, 2004.

Exercise 18-5
Stock appreciation rights; cash settlement

As part of its stock-based compensation package, National, Inc. granted 48,000 stock appreciation rights (SARs) to executives on January 1, 2003. At exercise, holders of the SARs are entitled to receive cash or stock equal in value to the excess of the market price at exercise over the share price at the date of grant. The SARs cannot be exercised until the end of 2005 (vesting date) and expire at the end of 2008. The common shares have a market price of $23 per share on the grant date. All recipients are expected to remain employed through the vesting date. The year-end share prices following the grant of the SARs are:

2003 – $25
2004 – $24
2005 – $25

Required:
1. Prepare the appropriate journal entry to record the award of SARs on January 1, 2003.
2. Prepare the appropriate journal entries pertaining to the SARs on December 31, 2003 – 2005.
3. The SARs are exercised on May 6, 2006, when the share price is $24, and executives choose to receive the market price appreciation in cash. Prepare the appropriate journal entry(ies) on that date.

EXERCISES

Exercise 19-1
Issuance of
shares; noncash
consideration

During its first year of operations, Yankee Communications entered into the following transactions relating to shareholders' equity. The articles of incorporation authorized the issue of 240 million common shares, $1 par per share, and 30 million preferred shares, $50 par per share.

Required:
Prepare the appropriate journal entries to record each transaction:

February 13   Sold 60 million common shares, for $10 per share.

February 14   Issued 1 million common shares to attorneys in exchange for legal services.

February 14   Sold 3 million of its common shares and 1 million preferred shares for $60 million.

November 16   Issued 190,000 of its common shares in exchange for equipment for which the cash price was known to be $1,844,000.

Exercise 19-2
Retirement of
shares

Brand Storage Company's articles of incorporation authorized the issuance of 520 million common shares. The transactions described below effected changes in Brand's outstanding shares. Prior to the transactions, Brand's shareholders' equity included the following:

Shareholders' Equity	$ in millions
Common stock, 400 million shares at $1 par, ...	$400
Paid-in capital – excess of par	1,200
Retained earnings	84

Required:
Assuming that Brand retires shares it reacquires (restores their status to that of authorized but unissued shares), record the appropriate journal entry for each of the following transactions:

a. On January 8, 2003, Brand reacquired 8 million shares at $6.00 per share.
b. On August 24, 2003, Brand reacquired 16 million shares at $5.50 per share.
c. On July 26, 2004, Brand sold 12 million common shares at $7.00 per share.

Exercise 19-3
Transactions
affecting retained
earnings

The balance sheet of MDS, Inc. included the following shareholders' equity accounts at December 31, 2002:

Paid-in capital:

Preferred stock, 7.6%, 100,000 shares at $1 par	$ 100,000
Common stock, 728,000 shares at $1 par	728,000
Paid-in capital – excess of par, preferred........	2,900,000
Paid-in capital – excess of par, common.........	5,148,000
Retained earnings..	9,800,000
Treasury stock, at cost; 8,000 common shares	(88,000)
Total shareholders' equity	$17,688,000

During 2003, several events and transactions affected the retained earnings of MDS.

Required:

1. Prepare the appropriate entries for these events.
    a. On February 20, the board of directors declared a property dividend of 100,000 shares of Brown International common stock that MDS had been purchased in January as an investment (book value: $485,000). The investment shares had a fair market value of $5 per share and were distributed March 20 to shareholders of record February 28.
    b. On April 4, a 5 for 4 stock split was declared and distributed. The stock split was effected in the form of a 25% stock dividend. The market value of the $1 par common stock was $12 per share.
    c. On July 25, a 3% common stock dividend was declared and distributed. The market value of the common stock was $12 per share.
    d. On December 2, the board of directors declared the 7.6% cash dividend on the 100,000 preferred shares, payable on December 27 to shareholders of record December 19.
    e. On December 2, the board of directors declared a cash dividend of $.50 per share on its common shares, payable on December 27 to shareholders of record December 19.
2. Prepare the shareholders' equity section of the balance sheet for MDS, Inc. for the year ended at December 31, 2003. Net income for the year was $900,000.

PROBLEMS

Problem 19-1
Share buybacks –
comparison of
retirement and
treasury stock

The shareholders' equity section of the balance sheet of Dodge, Inc. included the following accounts at December 31, 2002:

Shareholders' Equity	$ in millions
Common stock, 80 million shares at $1 par, ...	$ 80
Paid-in capital – excess of par	560
Paid-in capital – reacquired shares	1
Retained earnings	350

Required:

1. During 2003, Dodge reacquired shares of its common stock and later sold shares in two separate transactions. Prepare the entries for both the purchase and subsequent resale of shares, treated as both retired stock and treasury stock.
   a. On March 6, 2003, Dodge reacquired 3 million shares of stock at $10 per share.
   b. On September 3, 2003, the corporation sold 1 million shares at $11 per share.
   c. On October 12, 2005, the corporation sold 1 million shares at $4 per share.

2. Prepare the shareholders' equity section of Dodge's balance sheet at December 31, 2005, assuming Dodge retired the shares it reacquired and that Dodge treated reacquired shares as treasury stock. Assume all net income earned in 2003-2005 was distributed to shareholders as cash dividends.

Problem 19-2

Shareholders'
equity
transactions;
statement of
shareholders'
equity

Listed below are the transactions that affected the shareholders' equity of BLT Corporation during the period 2003 - 2005. At December 31, 2002, the corporation's accounts included:

	($ in 000s)
Common stock, 315 million shares at $1 par, ...	$315,000
Paid-in capital – excess of par	1,890,000
Retained earnings	2,910,000

a. November 2, 2003, the board of directors declared a cash dividend of $.80 per share on its common shares, payable to shareholders of record November 16, to be paid December 2.

b. On March 3, 2004, the board of directors declared a property dividend consisting of bonds of Blair County that BLT was holding as an investment. The bonds had a fair market value of $4.8 million, but were purchased two years previously for $3.9 million. Because they were intended to be held to maturity, the bonds had not been previously written up. The property dividend was payable to shareholders of record March 14, to be distributed April 6.

c. On July 13, 2004, the corporation declared and distributed a 5% common stock dividend (when the market value of the common stock was $21 per share). Cash was paid for fractional share rights representing 750,000 equivalent whole shares.

d. On November 2, 2004, the board of directors declared a cash dividend of $.80 per share on its common shares, payable to shareholders of record November 16, to be paid December 2.

e. On January 16, 2005, the board of directors declared and distributed a 3 for 2 stock split effected in the form of a 50% stock dividend when the market value of the common stock was $23 per share.

f. On November 2, 2005, the board of directors declared a cash dividend of $.65 per share on its common shares, payable to shareholders of record November 16, to be paid December 2.

Required:
1. Prepare the journal entries that BLT recorded during the three-year period for these transactions.
2. Prepare comparative statements of shareholders' equity for BLT for the three-year period ($ in 000s). Net income was $990 million, $1,185 million, and $1,365 million for 2003, 2004, and 2005, respectively.

EXERCISES

Exercise 20-1
Treasury stock; new shares; stock dividends; two years

The Reserve Company had 606 million shares of common stock outstanding at January 1, 2003. The following activities affected common shares during the year: There are no potential common shares outstanding.

2003
Feb. 27 Purchased 18 million shares of treasury stock.
Oct. 30 Sold the treasury shares purchased on February 27.
Nov. 29 Issued 72 million new shares.
Dec. 31 Net income for 2003 is $1,200 million.

2004
Jan. 14 Declared and issued a 2 for 1 stock split.
Dec. 31 Net income for 2004 is $1,200 million.

Required:
1. Determine the 2003 EPS.
2. Determine the 2004 EPS.
3. At what amount will the 2003 EPS be presented in the 2004 comparative financial statements?

PROBLEMS

Problem 20-1
Net loss; stock dividend; nonconvertible preferred stock; treasury shares; shares sold; extraordinary loss

On December 31, 2002, Parnell Corporation had 1,200,000 shares of common stock outstanding. Forty thousand shares of 7%, $100 par value cumulative, nonconvertible preferred stock were sold on January 2, 2003. On April 30, 2003, Parnell purchased 60,000 shares of its common stock as treasury stock. Twenty-four thousand treasury shares were sold on August 31. Parnell issued a 5% common stock dividend on June 12, 2003. No cash dividends were declared in 2003. For the year ended December 31, 2003, Parnell reported a net loss of $280,000, including an after-tax extraordinary loss of $800,000 from a litigation settlement.

Required:
1. Determine Parnell 's net loss per share for the year ended December 31, 2003.
2. Determine the per share amount of income or loss from continuing operations for the year ended December 31, 2003.
3. Prepare an EPS presentation that would be appropriate to appear on Ainsworth's 2003 and 2002 comparative income statements. Assume EPS were reported in 2002 as $.75, based on net income (no extraordinary items) of $900,000 and a weighted average number of common shares of 1,200,000.

Problem 20-2

On December 31, 2002, Warren Industries had 300 million shares of common stock and 2 million shares of 8%, noncumulative, nonconvertible preferred stock issued and outstanding. Warren issued a 4% common stock dividend on April 30 and paid cash dividends of $200 million and $39 million to common and preferred shareholders, respectively, on December 15, 2003.

On March 1, 2003, Warren sold 30 million common shares. In keeping with its long-term share repurchase plan, 2 million shares were retired on June 30. Warren's net income for the year ended December 31, 2003, was $1,050,000,000. The income tax rate is 40%.

Required:
Compute Warren 's earnings per share for the year ended December 31, 2003.

Problem 20-3

[Note: This is a variation of the previous problem, modified to include options, convertible bonds and contingently issuable shares.]

On December 31, 2002, Warren Industries had 300 million shares of common stock and 2 million shares of 8%, noncumulative, nonconvertible preferred stock issued and outstanding. Warren issued a 4% common stock dividend on April 30 and paid cash dividends of $200 million and $39 million to common and preferred shareholders, respectively, on December 15, 2003.

On March 1, 2003, Warren sold 30 million common shares. Also, as part of a 2002 agreement for the acquisition of RW, Inc., another 13 million shares (already adjusted for the stock dividend) are to be issued to former RW shareholders on December 31, 2004, if RW's 2004 net income is at least $250 million. In 2003, RW's net income was $290 million.

In keeping with its long-term share repurchase plan, 2 million shares were retired on June 30. Warren's net income for the year ended December 31, 2003, was $1,050,000,000. The income tax rate is 40%.

As part of an incentive compensation plan, Warren granted stock options to division managers at December 31 of the current and each of the previous two years. Each option permits its holder to buy one share of common stock at an exercise price equal to market value at the date of grant. Information concerning the number of options granted and common share prices follows:

Date granted	Options granted	Share price
	(adjusted for the stock dividend)	
December 31, 2001	2 million	$34
December 31, 2002	4 million	$24
December 31, 2003	3 million	$30

The market price of the common stock averaged $32 per share during 2003.

On July 12, 2004, Warren issued $400 million of convertible 10% bonds at face value. Each $1,000 bond is convertible into 30 common shares (adjusted for the stock dividend).

Required:
Compute Warren's basic and diluted earnings per share for the year ended December 31, 2003.

Problem 20-4

Options; convertible preferred; additional shares

On January 1, 2003, Buffy Industries had outstanding 880 million common shares (par $1) that originally sold for $19 per share, and 8 million shares of 10% cumulative preferred stock (par $100), convertible into 80 million common shares.

On September 30, 2003, Buffy sold and issued an additional 32 million shares of common stock at $38. At December 31, 2003, there were common stock options outstanding, issued in 2002, and exercisable for 40 million shares of common stock at an exercise price of $30. The market price of the common stock at year-end was $48. During the year the price of the common shares had averaged $40.

Net income was $1,300,000,000. The tax rate for the year was 40%.

Required:

Compute basic and diluted EPS for the year ended December 31, 2003.

$800 \times 10\% = 80$

$$\text{BASIC EPS} = \frac{1,300M - 80M}{880M + 32M \times {}^{3}/_{12}} = \frac{1,220M}{888M} = \$1.37$$

Diluted EPS   prefered stock incremental $= \dfrac{80M}{80M} = \$1.00$

$$\text{w/options} = \frac{1220}{888 + (40 - 40 \times \frac{30}{40})} = \frac{1220}{898}$$

$$= 1.36$$

$$\text{Diluted} = \frac{1220 + 80}{898 + 80} = \frac{1300}{978} = \$1.33$$

EXERCISES

Exercise 21-1
Change in accounting principle; change in depreciation methods

Bearing Products bought a machine at a total cost of $105,000 million in 2000. The machine was being depreciated over a 10-year life using the sum-of-the-years'-digits method. The residual value is expected to be $6,000. At the beginning of 2003 Bearing decided to change to the straight-line method.

Required:
Prepare all appropriate journal entry(s) relating to the machine for 2003. (Ignore income tax effects.)

Exercise 21-2
Change in inventory costing methods

In 2004, the Emerson, Inc. changed its method of valuing inventory from the FIFO method to the average cost method. At December 31, 2003, Emerson's inventories were $96,000 (FIFO). Emerson's records indicated that the inventories would have totaled $71,400 at December 31, 2003, if determined on an average cost basis.

Required:
1. Prepare the journal entry to record the adjustment. (Ignore income taxes.)
2. Briefly describe other steps Emerson should take to report the change.

Exercise 21-3
Warranty expense

Key Services introduced a new line of lawn products in 2003 that carry a one-year warranty against manufacturer's defects. Because this was the first product for which the company offered a warranty, trade publications were consulted to determine the experience of others in the industry. Based on that experience, warranty costs were expected to approximate 3% of sales. Sales of the sprinklers in 2003 were $500,000. Accordingly, the following entries relating to the contingency for warranty costs were recorded during the first year of selling the product:

Accrued liability and expense
Warranty expense (3% x $500,000)   15,000
    Estimated warranty liability
    15,000

Actual expenditures (summary entry)
Estimated warranty liability ...   4,600
    Cash, wages payable, parts and supplies, etc.   4,600

In late 2004, the company's claims experience was evaluated and it was determined that claims were far more than expected – 4% of sales rather than 3%.

Required:
1. Assuming sales of the sprinklers in 2004 were $720,000 and warranty expenditures in 2004 totaled $17,600, prepare any journal entries related to the warranty.
2. Assuming sales of the sprinklers were discontinued after 2003, prepare any journal entry(s) in 2004 related to the warranty.

PROBLEMS

Problem 21-1
Accounting changes; six situations

Described below are six independent and unrelated situations involving accounting changes. Each change occurs during 2003 before any adjusting entries or closing entries were prepared. Assume the tax rate for each company is 40% in all years. Any tax effects should be adjusted through the deferred tax liability account.

a. JB Industries introduced a new line of auto covers in 2002 that carry a one-year warranty against manufacturer's defects. Based on industry experience, warranty costs were expected to approximate 4% of sales. Sales of the covers in 2002 were $700,000. Accordingly, warranty expense and a warranty liability of $28,000 were recorded in 2002. In late 2003, the company's claims experience was evaluated and it was determined that claims were far fewer than expected: 3% of sales rather than 4%. Sales of the covers in 2003 were $800,000 and warranty expenditures in 2003 totaled $18,000

b. On December 30, 1999, Jefferson, Inc. acquired its office building at a cost of $4,000,000. It has been depreciated on a straight-line basis assuming a useful life of 40 years and no salvage value. However, plans were finalized in 2003 to relocate the company headquarters at the end of 2010. The vacated office building will have a salvage value at that time of $2,800,000.

c. Sterling Technology changed inventory cost methods to LIFO from FIFO at the end of 2003 for both financial statement and income tax purposes. Under FIFO, the inventory at January 1, 2004, is $13 million.

d. At the beginning of 1999, DD Corp. purchased office equipment at a cost of $990,000. Its useful life was estimated to be ten years with no salvage value. The equipment has been depreciated by the sum-of-the-years'-digits method. On January 1, 2003, the company changed to the straight-line method.

e. In October, 2001, the State of Florida filed suit against Master Industries, seeking penalties for violations of clean air laws. When the financial statements were issued in 2002, Master had not reached a settlement with state authorities, but legal counsel advises Master that it was probable the company would have to pay $40 million in penalties. Accordingly, the following entry was recorded:

Loss – litigation 40,000,000
    Liability - litigation 40,000,000

Late in 2003, a settlement was reached with state authorities to pay a total of $45 million in penalties.

f. At the beginning of 2003, the Higher Tech, which uses the sum-of-the-years'-digits method changed to the straight-line method for newly acquired equipment. The change increased current year net earnings by $4.6 million.

Required:
For each situation:
- Identify the type of change.
- Prepare any journal entry necessary as a direct result of the change as well as any adjusting entry for 2003 related to the situation described.

- Briefly describe any other steps that should be taken to appropriately report the situation.

Problem 21-2
Correction of errors; six errors

Lawrence-Gabe Storage underwent a restructuring in 2003. The company conducted a thorough internal audit, during which the following facts were discovered. The audit occurred during 2003 before any adjusting entries or closing entries are prepared.

a. Additional printers were acquired at the beginning of 2001 and added to the company's office network. The $9,000 cost of the printers was inadvertently recorded as maintenance expense. The printers have five-year useful lives and no material salvage value. This class of equipment is depreciated by the straight-line method.

b. Three weeks prior to the audit, the company paid $51,000 for storage boxes and recorded the expenditure as office supplies. The error was discovered a week later.

c. On December 31, 2002, inventory was understated by $112,000 due to a mistake in the physical inventory count. The company uses the periodic inventory system.

d. Three years earlier, the company recorded a 3% stock dividend (4,000 common shares, $1 par) as follows:

Retained earnings	4,000	
Common stock		4,000

The shares had a market price at the time of $10 per share.

e. At the end of 1999, the company failed to accrue $60,000 of interest expense that accrued during the last four month's of 2002 on bonds payable. The bonds which were issued at face value mature in 2007. The following entry was recorded on March 1, 2003, when the semiannual interest was paid:

Interest expense	180,000	
Cash		180,000

f. A three-year liability insurance policy was purchased at the beginning of 2002 for $216,000. The full premium was debited to insurance expense at the time.

Required:
For each error, prepare any journal entry necessary to correct the error as well as any year-end adjusting entry for 2003 related to the situation described. (Ignore income taxes.)

EXERCISES

Exercise 22-1
Summary entries for cash paid to suppliers of merchandise

For each of the five independent situations below, prepare the summary entry that determines the amount of cash paid to suppliers and explains the change in each account shown. All dollars are in millions.

Situation	Cost of goods sold	Inventory increase (decrease)	Accounts payable increase (decrease)	Cash paid to suppliers
1	600	0	0	?
2	600	18	0	?
3	600	0	42	?
4	600	18	42	?
5	600	(18)	(42)	?

1. Cost of Goods Sold   600
        CASH   600

2. Cost of Goods Sold   600
   Inventory   18
        CASH   618

4. Cost of Goods Sold   600
   Inventory   18
        Accounts Payable   42
        CASH   576

3. Cost of Goods Sold   600
        Accounts Payable   42
        CASH   558

5. Cost of Goods Sold   600
   Accounts Payable   42
        Inventory   18
        CASH   624

Exercise 22-2
Reconciliation of
Net Cash Flows
From Operating
Activities to Net
Income

The income statement and the "cash flows from operating activities" section of the statement of cash flows are provided below for Robert Mathis Company. The merchandise inventory account balance neither increased nor decreased during the reporting period. Mathis had no liability for either insurance, deferred income taxes, or interest at any time during the period.

Robert Mathis Company
INCOME STATEMENT
For the Year Ended December 31, 2003 ($ in millions)

Sales		$936
Cost of goods sold		(564)
Gross margin		$372
Salaries expense	$123	
Insurance expense	66	
Depreciation expense	33	
Depletion expense	15	
Bond interest expense	30	(267)
Gains and losses:		
Gain on sale of equipment		75
Loss on sale of land		(24)
Income before tax		$ 156
Income tax expense		(78)
Net Income		$ 78

Cash Flows From Operating Activities:

Cash received from customers	$774
Cash paid to suppliers	(525)
Cash paid to employees	(111)
Cash paid for interest	(27)
Cash paid for insurance	(48)
Cash paid for income taxes	(42)
Net cash flows from operating activities	$21

Required:
Prepare a schedule to reconcile Net Income to Net Cash Flows From Operating Activities.

Reconciliation of Net Income To Net Cash Flows from Operating
Activities:

Net Income 78
Adjustments For Non-Cash Effects:
Increase in Accounts Receivable (162)
Increase in Accounts Payable 39
Increase in Salaries Payable 12
Decrease in Prepaid Insurance 18
Depreciation 33
Depletion 15
Decrease in Bond Discount 3
Gain on Equipment (75)
Loss on Land 24
Income taxes Payable 36
21

Exercise 22-3
Cash Flows From Operating Activities (direct method) derived from an income statement and Cash Flows From Operating Activities (indirect method)

The income statement and a schedule reconciling "cash flows from operating activities" to net income are provided below ($ in 000) for Sun Technologies.

<table>
<tr><td colspan="3">Sun Technologies
Income Statement
For The Year Ended
December 31, 2003</td><td colspan="2">Reconciliation Of
Net Income To
Net Cash Flows
From Operating Activities</td></tr>
<tr><td>Sales</td><td></td><td>$915</td><td>Net income</td><td>$66</td></tr>
<tr><td>Cost of goods sold</td><td></td><td>(555)</td><td></td><td></td></tr>
<tr><td>Gross margin</td><td></td><td>$360</td><td>Adjustments for noncash effects:</td><td></td></tr>
<tr><td>Salaries expense</td><td>$123</td><td></td><td>Depreciation expense</td><td>33</td></tr>
<tr><td>Insurance expense</td><td>57</td><td></td><td>Loss on sale of land</td><td>15</td></tr>
<tr><td>Depreciation expense</td><td>33</td><td></td><td>Decrease in accounts receivable</td><td>18</td></tr>
<tr><td>Loss on sale of land</td><td>15</td><td>228</td><td>Increase in inventory</td><td>(39)</td></tr>
<tr><td>Income before tax</td><td></td><td>$132</td><td>Decrease in accounts payable</td><td>(24)</td></tr>
<tr><td>Income tax expense</td><td></td><td>(66)</td><td>Increase in salaries payable</td><td>15</td></tr>
<tr><td>Net Income</td><td></td><td>$ 66</td><td>Decrease in prepaid insurance</td><td>27</td></tr>
<tr><td></td><td></td><td></td><td>Increase in income tax payable</td><td>60</td></tr>
<tr><td></td><td></td><td></td><td>Net cash flows from
operating activities</td><td>$171</td></tr>
</table>

Required:
1. Calculate each of the following amounts for Sun Technologies:
   a. Cash received from customers during the reporting period.
   b. Cash paid to suppliers of goods during the reporting period.
   c. Cash paid to employees during the reporting period.
   d. Cash paid for insurance during the reporting period.
   e. Cash paid for income taxes during the reporting period.
2. Prepare the "Cash Flows From Operating Activities" section of the statement of cash flows (direct method).

Exercise 22-4
Indirect method; reconciliation of net income to net cash flows from operating

The accounting records of Close Company provided the data below:

Net loss	$25,000
Depreciation expense	30,000
Increase in salaries payable	2,500
Decrease in accounts receivable	10,000
Increase in inventory	11,500
Amortization of patent	1,500
Reduction in discount on bonds	1,000

Required:
Prepare a reconciliation of net income to net cash flows from operating activities.

PROBLEMS

Problem 22-1
Classifications of
Cash Flows From
Investing and
Financing
Activities

Listed below are transactions that might be reported as investing and/or financing activities on a statement of cash flows. Possible reporting classifications of those transactions are provided also.

Classifications

+ I	Investing activity (cash inflow)
– I	Investing activity (cash outflow
+ F	Financing activity (cash inflow)
– F	Financing activity (cash outflow)
N	Noncash investing and financing activity
X	Not reported as an investing and/or a financing activity

Transactions

Example **+ I**   1. Sale of a building
+ F   2. Issuance of preferred stock for cash
– F   3. Retirement of preferred stock
N   4. Conversion of bonds to common stock
N   5. Lease of a machine by capital lease
+ I   6. Sale of a trademark
– I   7. Purchase of land for cash
N   8. Issuance of common stock for a building
+ I   9. Collection of a note receivable (principal amount)
+ F 10. Sale of bonds payable
X 11. Distribution of a stock dividend
N 12. Payment of property dividend
– F 13. Payment of cash dividends
+ F 14. Issuance of a short-term note payable for cash
+ F 15. Issuance of a long-term note payable for cash
– I 16. Purchase of investment securities (not cash equivalent)
– F 17. Repayment of a note payable
X 18. Cash payment for 3-year insurance policy
+ I 19. Sale of land
N 20. Issuance of note payable for land
– I 21. Purchase of common stock issued by another corporation
N 22. Repayment of long-term debt by issuing common stock
X 23. Restriction of retained earnings for plant expansion
X 24. Payment of semiannual interest on notes payable
– F 25. Purchase of treasury stock
– I 26. Loan to a subsidiary
X 27. Sale of merchandise to customers
X 28. Purchase of treasury bills (cash equivalents)

Problem 22-2
Statement of cash flows; direct method; use spreadsheet

Comparative balance sheets for 2003 and 2002 and an income statement for 2003 are provided below for A2Z Industries. Additional information from the accounting records of A2Z also is provided.

A2Z Industries
Comparative Balance Sheets
December 31, 2003 and 2002 ($ in 000)

	2003	2002
Assets:		
Cash	$ 1,800	$ 1,125
Accounts receivable	1,800	1,350
Inventory	2,700	1,575
Land	2,025	1,800
Building	2,700	2,700
Less: Accumulated depreciation	(900)	(810)
Equipment	8,550	6,750
Less: Accumulated depreciation	(1,575)	(1,440)
Patent	3,600	4,500
	$20,700	$17,550
Liabilities:		
Accounts payable	$ 2,250	$ 1,350
Accrued expenses payable	900	675
Lease liability – land	450	0
Shareholders' Equity:		
Common stock	9,450	9,000
Paid-in capital - excess of par	2,250	2,025
Retained earnings	5,400	4,500
	$20,700	$17,550

A2Z Industries
Income Statement
For year ended December 31, 2003 ($ in 000)

Revenues:		
Sales revenue	$7,935	
Gain on sale of land	270	$8,205
Expenses:		
Cost of goods sold	$1,800	
Depreciation expense-building	90	
Depreciation expense-equipment	945	
Loss on sale of equipment	45	
Amortization of patent	900	
Operating expenses	1,500	5,280
Net income		$2,925

Additional information from the accounting records:

a. During 2003, equipment with a cost of $900,000 (90% depreciated) was sold.

b. The Statement of Shareholders' Equity reveals reductions of $675,000 and $1,350,000 for stock dividends and cash dividends, respectively.

Required:

Prepare the statement of cash flows of A2Z for the year ended December 31, 2003. Present "cash flows from operating activities" by the direct method and use a spreadsheet to assist in your analysis. [You may omit the schedule to reconcile net income with cash flows from operating activities.]

Problem 22-3
Statement of cash flows; indirect method

Refer to the data provided in the previous problem for A2Z Industries.

Required:

Prepare the statement of cash flows for A2Z Industries using the *indirect method.*

Part II

Solutions

Chapter 1   Environment and Theoretical Structure of Financial Accounting

EXERCISES

Exercise 1-1

Requirement 1

	Haskins and Price **Operating Cash Flow**	
	Year 1	**Year 2**
Cash collected	$330,000	$450,000
Cash disbursements:		
Payment of rent	(60,000)	- 0 -
Salaries	(200,000)	(210,000)
Travel	(50,000)	(60,000)
Utilities	(30,000)	(50,000
Net operating cash flow	$(10,000)	$130,000

Requirement 2

	Haskins and Price **Income Statements**	
	Year 1	**Year 2**
Revenues	$380,000	$440,000
Expenses:		
Salaries	(200,000)	(210,000)
Utilities	(40,000)	(40,000)
Travel	(50,000)	(60,000)
Rent	(30,000)	(30,000)
Net Income	$ 60,000	$100,000

Requirement 3

Year 1:	Amounts billed to customers	$380,000
	Less: Cash collected	(330,000)
	Ending accounts receivable	$ 50,000

Year 2:	Beginning accounts receivable	$ 50,000
	Plus: Amounts billed to customers	440,000
		$490,000
	Less: Cash collected	(450,000)
	Ending accounts receivable	$ 40,000

Exercise 1-2

	List A	List B
g	1. predictive value	a. applying the same accounting practices over time
h	2. relevance	b. record expenses in the period the related revenue is recognized
e	3. reliability	c. concerns the relative size of an item and its effect on decisions
j	4. comprehensive income	d. concerns the recognition of revenue
c	5. materiality	e. along with relevance, a primary decision-specific quality
a	6. consistency	f. the original transaction value upon acquisition
i	7. verifiability	g. information is useful in predicting the future
b	8. matching principle	h. pertinent to the decision at hand
f	9. historical cost principle	i. implies consensus among different measurers
d	10. realization principle	j. the change in equity from nonowner transactions

Exercise 1-3

1. The periodicity assumption
2. The matching principle
3. The historical cost or original transaction value principle
4. The full disclosure principle
5. The realization principle or revenue recognition principle
6. The economic entity assumption

Exercise 1-4

1. The periodicity assumption
2. The historical cost or original transaction value principle
3. The matching principle
4. The full disclosure principle
5. The economic entity assumption
6. The realization principle or revenue recognition principle

EXERCISES

Exercise 2-1

	Assets		=	Liabilities + Paid-in Capital + Retained Earnings

	Assets		Liabilities + Paid-in Capital	Retained Earnings
1.	+ 800,000	(cash)	+ 800,000 (common stock)	
2.	- 15,000	(cash)		
	+ 60,000	(equipment)	+ 45,000 (note payable)	
3.	+ 270,000	(inventory)	+ 270,000 (accounts payable)	
4.	+ 360,000	(accounts receivable)		+ 360,000 (revenue)
	- 210,000	(inventory)		- 210,000 (expense)
5.	- 20,000	(cash)		- 20,000 (expense)
6.	- 15,000	(cash)		
	+ 15,000	(prepaid insurance)		
7.	- 180,000	(cash)	- 180,000 (accounts payable)	
8.	+ 190,000	(cash)		
	- 190,000	(accounts receivable)		
9.	- 2,000	(accumulated depreciation)		- 2,000 (expense)

Exercise 2-2

1.	Cash	800,000	
	Common stock		800,000
2.	Equipment	60,000	
	Note payable		45,000
	Cash		15,000
3.	Inventory	270,000	
	Accounts payable		270,000
4.	Accounts receivable	360,000	
	Sales revenue		360,000
	Cost of goods sold	210,000	
	Inventory		210,000
5.	Rent expense	20,000	
	Cash		20,000
6.	Prepaid insurance	15,000	
	Cash		15,000
7.	Accounts payable	180,000	
	Cash		180,000
8.	Cash	190,000	
	Accounts receivable		190,000
9.	Depreciation expense	2,000	
	Accumulated depreciation		2,000

Exercise 2-3

	Increase (I) or Decrease (D)	Account
1.	D	Accounts receivable
2.	D	Salary expense
3.	D	Loss on sale of land
4.	D	Prepaid insurance
5.	I	Interest revenue
6.	I	Common stock
7.	I	Interest payable
8.	D	Land
9.	D	Interest expense
10.	I	Gain on sale of equipment
11.	D	Interest expense
12.	I	Accumulated depreciation
13.	D	Bad debt expense
14.	I	Sales revenue

Exercise 2-4

		Account(s) Debited	Account(s) Credited
Example:	Purchased equipment for cash	2	5
1.	Paid a cash dividend.	10	5
2.	Paid insurance for the next six months.	8	5
3.	Sold goods to customers on account.	4,16	9,3
4.	Purchased inventory for cash.	3	5
5.	Purchased supplies on account.	6	1
6.	Paid employees wages for November.	17	5
7.	Issued common stock in exchange for cash.	5	12
8.	Collected cash from customers on account.	5	4
9.	Borrowed cash from a bank and signed a note.	5	11
10.	At the end of November, recorded the amount of supplies that had been used during the month.	7	6
11.	Paid October's interest on a bank loan.	13	5
12.	Accrued interest expense for November.	18	13

Exercise 2-5

1. Insurance expense ($12,000 x $5/24$).............................	2,500	
Prepaid insurance		2,500
2. Depreciation expense..	20,000	
Accumulated depreciation		20,000
3. Salaries expense..	27,000	
Salaries payable		27,000
4. Interest receivable ($50,000 x 8% x $3/12$)....................	1,000	
Interest revenue...		1,000
5. Supplies	2,200	
Supplies expense..		2,200

Exercise 2-6

Requirement 1

Supplies			
11/30 Balance	4,000		
		Expense	?
Purchased	6,000		
12/31 Balance	8,000		

Cost of supplies used = $4,000 + 6,000 - 8,000 = **$2,000**

Requirement 2

Prepaid rent			
11/30 Balance	10,000		
		Expense	?
12/31 Balance	7,000		

Rent expense for December = $10,000 – 7,000 = **$3,000**

Exercise 2-6 (concluded)

Requirement 3

	Interest payable	
		7,000	11/30 Balance
Interest paid	?	2,000	Accrued interest
		4,000	12/31 Balance

Cash paid during December = $7,000 + 2,000 − 4,000 = **$5,000**

Requirement 4

	Unearned rent revenue	
		4,500	11/30 Balance
Earned for Dec. 1,500			
		3,000	12/31 Balance

Rent revenue recognized each month = $6,000 \times \frac{1}{4}$ = **$1,500**

December 31, 2003

Unearned rent revenue	1,500	
Rent revenue		1,500

PROBLEMS

Problem 2-1

Requirement 1

2003		Debit	Credit
July 1	Cash	1,000,000	
	Common stock		1,000,000
July 2	Inventory	80,000	
	Accounts payable		80,000
July 4	Prepaid rent	10,000	
	Cash		10,000
July 10	Accounts receivable	120,000	
	Sales revenue		120,000
July 10	Cost of goods sold	75,000	
	Inventory		75,000
July 15	Cash	50,000	
	Note payable		50,000
July 20	Wages expense	15,000	
	Cash		15,000
July 24	Accounts payable	50,000	
	Cash		50,000
July 26	Cash	60,000	
	Accounts receivable		60,000
July 28	Utilities expense	1,500	
	Cash		1,500
July 31	Prepaid insurance	8,000	
	Cash		8,000

Problem 2-1 *(continued)*

Requirement 2

Cash

7/1 Bal.	0		
7/1	1,000,000	10,000	7/4
7/15	50,000	15,000	7/20
7/26	60,000	50,000	7/24
		1,500	7/28
		8,000	7/31
7/31 Bal.	1,025,500		

Accounts receivable

7/1 Bal.	0		
7/10	120,000	60,000	7/26
7/31 Bal.	60,000		

Inventory

7/1 Bal.	0		
7/2	80,000	75,000	7/10
7/31 Bal.	5,000		

Prepaid insurance

7/1 Bal.	0	
7/31	8,000	
7/31 Bal.	8,000	

Prepaid rent

7/1 Bal.	0	
7/4	10,000	
7/31 Bal.	10,000	

Accounts payable

		0	7/1 Bal.
7/24	50,000	80,000	7/2
		30,000	**7/31 Bal.**

Note payable

	0	7/1 Bal.
	50,000	7/15
	50,000	**7/31 Bal.**

Common stock

	0	7/1 Bal.
	1,000,000	7/1
	1,000,000	**7/31 Bal.**

Problem 2-1 (concluded)

INCOME STATEMENT ACCOUNTS

Sales revenue

	0	7/1 Bal.
	120,000	7/10
	120,000	**7/31 Bal.**

Cost of goods sold

7/1 Bal.	0	
7/10	75,000	
7/31 Bal.	75,000	

Utilities expense

7/1 Bal.	0	
7/28	1,500	
7/31 Bal.	1,500	

Wages expense

7/1 Bal.	0	
7/20	15,000	
7/31 Bal.	15,000	

Requirement 3

Account Title	Debits	Credits
Cash	1,025,500	
Accounts receivable	60,000	
Inventory	5,000	
Prepaid rent	10,000	
Prepaid insurance	8,000	
Accounts payable		30,000
Note payable		50,000
Common stock		1,000,000
Sales revenue		120,000
Cost of goods sold	75,000	
Wages expense	15,000	
Utilities expense	1,500	
Totals	1,200,000	1,200,000

Problem 2-2

1. Depreciation expense 22,000
      Accumulated depreciation   22,000
2. Wage expense ($7,000 – 5,000).................................. 2,000
      Wages payable   2,000
3. Interest expense ($50,000 x 8% x $9/12) 3,000
      Interest payable   3,000
4. Supplies expense ($2,300 – 1,000) 1,300
      Supplies   1,300
5. Unearned revenue 3,000
      Sales revenue   3,000
6. Rent expense... 1,000
      Prepaid rent   1,000

Chapter 3 The Balance Sheet and Financial Disclosures

EXERCISES

Exercise 3-1

1. __b__ Note receivable, due in 2 years
2. __a__ Accounts receivable
3. __-c__ Accumulated depreciation
4. __c__ Land, in use
5. __f__ Note payable, due in 10 months
6. __f__ Interest payable
7. __a__ Note receivable, due in 6 months
8. __a__ Cash equivalents
9. __b__ Investment in ABC Corp., long-term

10. __a__ Inventories
11. __d__ Goodwill
12. __f__ Accrued salaries payable
13. __f__ Accrued taxes payable
14. __a__ Prepaid insurance
15. __h__ Common stock
16. __c__ Equipment
17. __f__ Unearned revenue
18. __f__ Warranties payable

Exercise 3-2

CURTIS CORPORATION
Balance Sheet
At December 31, 2003

Assets

Current assets:

Cash and cash equivalents	$ 70,000
Marketable securities	15,000
Accounts receivable	110,000
Interest receivable	2,000
Inventories	120,000
Prepaid insurance	3,000
Total current assets	320,000

Investments and funds:

Note receivable	50,000

Property, plant, and equipment:

Machinery and equipment	$230,000	
Less: Accumulated depreciation	(111,000)	
Net property, plant, and equipment		119,000
Total assets		$489,000

Liabilities and Shareholders' Equity

Current liabilities:

Accounts payable	$ 45,000
Wages payable	10,000
Interest payable	3,000
Total current liabilities	58,000

Long-term liabilities:

Bonds payable	100,000

Shareholders' equity:

Common stock	$200,000	
Retained earnings	131,000	
Total shareholders' equity		331,000
Total liabilities and shareholders' equity		$489,000

Exercise 3-3

1. Depreciation method — A
2. Information on related party transactions — B
3. Method of accounting for acquisitions — A
4. Composition and details of long-term debt — B
5. Inventory method — A
6. Basis of revenue recognition — A
7. Major damage to a plant facility occurring after year-end — B
8. Composition of accrued liabilities — B

Exercise 3-4

1. Current ratio — $[\$150 + 400 + 500] \div \$600 = 1.75$
2. Acid-test ratio — $[\$150 + 400] \div \$600 = .92$
3. Debt to equity ratio — $[\$600 + 500] \div [\$1,000 + 150] = .96$
4. Times interest earned ratio — $[\$260 + 30 + 200] \div \$30 = 16.3$ times

Exercise 3-5

Action	Current Ratio	Acid-test Ratio	Debt to Equity Ratio
1. Issuance of common stock for cash	I	I	D
2. Purchase of inventory on account	I	D	I
3. Receipt of cash from a customer on account	N	N	N
4. Expiration of prepaid rent	D	N	I
5. Payment of a cash dividend	D	D	I
6. Purchase of equipment with a 6-month note	D	D	I
7. Purchase of long-term investment for cash	D	D	N
8. Sale of equipment for cash (no gain or loss)	I	I	N
9. Write-off of obsolete inventory	D	N	I
10. Decision to refinance on a long-term basis currently-maturing debt	I	I	N

PROBLEMS
Problem 3-1

ALEXANDRIA EXPLORATION CORPORATION
Balance Sheet
At December 31, 2003

Assets

Current assets:

Cash and cash equivalents		$ 62,000
Short-term investments		130,000
Accounts receivable, net of allowance for uncollectible accounts of $15,000		155,000
Interest receivable		3,000
Inventories		200,000
Supplies		3,000
Total current assets		553,000

Investments:

Land held for sale	$ 20,000	
Note receivable	50,000	
Total investments		70,000

Property, plant, and equipment:

Land	80,000	
Buildings	500,000	
Machinery	250,000	
	830,000	
Less: Accumulated depreciation	(230,000)	
Net property, plant, and equipment		600,000

Intangibles:

Goodwill		36,000
Total assets		$1,259,000

Liabilities and Shareholders' Equity

Current liabilities:

Accounts payable		$ 125,000
Interest payable		40,000
Bonds payable		200,000
Total current liabilities		365,000

Long-term liabilities:

Bonds payable		300,000

Shareholders' equity:

Common stock, no par value; 1,000,000 shares authorized; 500,000 shares issued and outstanding	500,000	
Retained earnings	94,000	
Total shareholders' equity		594,000
Total liabilities and shareholders' equity		$1,259,000

Problem 3-2

TILLAMOO CHEESE COMPANY
Balance Sheet
At December 31, 2003

Assets

Current assets:

Cash and cash equivalents		$ 190,000
Investment in stocks		40,000
Accounts receivable		300,000
Inventories		235,000
Prepaid expenses		15,000
Total current assets		780,000

Investments:

Investment in bonds		260,000

Property, plant, and equipment:

Land	$ 950,000	
Buildings	1,200,000	
Equipment	900,000	
	3,050,000	
Less: Accumulated depreciation	(600,000)	
Net property, plant, and equipment		2,450,000

Intangibles:

Patent	80,000	
Goodwill	220,000	
Total intangibles		300,000
Total assets		$3,790,000

Liabilities and Shareholders' Equity

Current liabilities:

Accounts payable		$ 260,000
Interest payable		20,000
Other accrued liabilities		60,000
Notes payable		180,000
Total current liabilities		520,000

Long-term liabilities:

Notes payable	100,000	
Bonds payable	1,000,000	
Total long-term liabilities		1,100,000

Shareholders' equity:

Common stock	1,500,000	
Retained earnings	670,000	
Total shareholders' equity		2,170,000
Total liabilities and shareholders' equity		$3,790,000

EXERCISES

Exercise 4-1

Requirement 1

APEX COMPUTER CORPORATION
Income Statement
For the Year Ended December 31, 2003

Revenues and gains:

Sales		$3,400,000
Interest revenue		35,000
Gain on sale of equipment		30,000
Total revenues and gains		3,465,000

Expenses and losses:

Cost of goods sold	$2,250,000	
Administrative expense	450,000	
Selling expense	150,000	
Restructuring costs	400,000	
Interest expense	20,000	
Income tax expense *	78,000	
Total expenses and losses		3,348,000
Income before extraordinary item		117,000
Extraordinary item:		
Loss from hurricane damage (net of $120,000 tax benefit)		(180,000)
Net loss		$ (63,000)

Earnings per share:

Income before extraordinary item	$ .23
Extraordinary item	(.36)
Net loss	$.(13)

---

* 40% x $195,000

Exercise 4-1 (concluded)

Requirement 2

APEX COMPUTER CORPORATION
Income Statement
For the Year Ended December 31, 2003

Sales revenue		$3,400,000
Cost of goods sold		2,250,000
Gross profit		1,150,000
Operating expenses:		
Administrative expense	$450,000	
Selling expense	150,000	
Restructuring costs	400,000	
Total operating expenses		1,000,000
Operating income		150,000
Other income (expense):		
Interest revenue	35,000	
Gain on sale of equipment	30,000	
Interest expense	(20,000)	
Total other income (expense), net		45,000
Income from continuing operations before		
income taxes		195,000
Income tax expense *		78,000
Income before extraordinary item		117,000
Extraordinary item:		
Loss from hurricane damage (net of $120,000 tax		
benefit)		(180,000)
Net loss		$ (63,000)
Earnings per share:		
Income before extraordinary item		$ .23
Extraordinary item		(.36)
Net loss		$.(13)

---

* 40% x $195,000

Exercise 4-2

BILIBONG COMPANY
Income Statement
For the Year Ended December 31, 2003

Income from continuing operations	$ 500,000
Discontinued operations:	
Loss from operations of discontinued component	
(including gain on disposal of $300,000) *	(80,000)
Income tax benefit	32,000
Loss on discontinued operations	(48,000)
Net income	$ 452,000
Earnings per share:	
Income from continuing operations	$ 2.50
Loss from discontinued operations	(.24)
Net income	$ 2.26

---

* Loss on discontinued operations:

Gain on sale of assets	$300,000
Operating loss	(380,000)
Total before tax loss	(80,000)
Less: Income tax benefit (40%)	32,000
Net of tax loss	$ (48,000)

Exercise 4-3

Requirement 1

OTTOBONI CORPORATION
Income Statement
For the Year Ended December 31, 2003

Income from continuing operations	$600,000
Discontinued operations:	
Loss from operations of discontinued component	
(including impairment loss of $200,000) *	(470,000)
Income tax benefit	188,000
Loss on discontinued operations	(282,000)
Net income	$318,000

* Loss on discontinued operations:

Operating loss	$ (270,000)
Impairment loss ($2,100,000 – 1,900,000)	(200,000)
Net before-tax loss	(470,000)
Income tax benefit (40%)	188,000
Net after-tax estimated loss on discontinued operations	$ (282,000)

Requirement 2

OTTOBONI CORPORATION
Income Statement
For the Year Ended December 31, 2003

Income from continuing operations	$600,000
Discontinued operations:	
Loss from operations of discontinued component *	(270,000)
Income tax benefit	108,000
Loss on discontinued operations	(162,000)
Net income	$438,000

* Includes only the operating loss during the year. There is no impairment loss.

Exercise 4-4

Requirement 1

When an estimate is revised as new information comes to light, accounting for the change in estimate is quite straightforward. We do not restate prior years' financial statements to reflect the new estimate; nor do we report the cumulative effect of the change in current income. Instead, we merely incorporate the new estimate in any related accounting determinations from there on. If the after-tax income effect of the change in estimate is material, the effect on net income and earnings per share must be disclosed in a note, along with the justification for the change.

Requirement 2

	$2,500,000	Cost
$400,000		Old annual depreciation ([$2,500,000 – 100,000] ÷ 6 years)
x 1.5 years	600,000	Depreciation to date (2001-2002)
	1,900,000	Book value
	(200,000)	Less new salvage value
	1,700,000	Revised depreciable base
	÷ 8.5	Estimated remaining life (10 years – 1.5 years)
	$ 200,000	New annual depreciation

Exercise 4-5

1.	d	Purchase of equipment in exchange for a note payable.
2.	a	Payment of rent.
3.	a	Collection of cash from customers.
4.	a	Payment of interest on debt.
5.	b	Purchase of a bond of another company.
6.	c	Issuance of common stock for cash.
7.	b	Sale of land for cash.
8.	a	Receipt of interest on a note receivable.
9.	b	Receipt of principal on a note receivable.
10.	c	Payment of cash dividends to shareholders.
11.	a	Payment to suppliers of inventory.

PROBLEMS

Problem 4-1

AJAX COMPANY
Income Statement
For the Year Ended December 31, 2003

Sales revenue		$6,200,000
Cost of goods sold		3,500,000
Gross profit		2,700,000
Operating expenses:		
Administrative and selling	$1,500,000	
Restructuring costs	250,000	
Loss from landslide damage	75,000	
Total operating expenses		1,825,000
Operating income		875,000
Other income (expense):		
Interest revenue	100,000	
Interest expense	(150,000)	
Loss on sale of equipment	(40,000)	(90,000)
Income from continuing operations before		
income taxes		785,000
Income tax expense		314,000
Income from continuing operations		471,000
Extraordinary item:		
Gain on sale of land (net of $800,000 tax benefit)		1,200,000
Net income		$1,671,000

Note:
1. The restructuring costs are not an extraordinary item.
2. The loss caused by the landslide is not an extraordinary item.

Problem 4-2

Requirement 1

HUNTINGTON STEEL CORPORATION
Comparative Income Statements
For the Years Ended December 31

	2003	2002
Income from continuing operations before income taxes [1]	$4,355,000	$3,475,000
Income tax expense	1,742,000	1,390,000
Income from continuing operations	2,613,000	2,085,000
Discontinued operations:		
Income from operations of discontinued component (including gain on disposal of $800,000 in 2003) [2]	345,000	325,000
Income tax expense	138,000	130,000
Income on discontinued operations	207,000	195,000
Net Income	$2,820,000	$2,280,000

[1] Income from continuing operations before income taxes:

	2003	2002
Unadjusted	$3,900,000	$3,800,000
Add: Loss from discontinued operation	455,000	
Deduct: Income from discontinued operation		(325,000)
Adjusted	$4,355,000	$3,475,000

[2] Income from discontinued operations:

	2003	2002
Operating income (loss)	$(455,000)	$ 325,000
Gain on disposal	800,000	-
Total	$ 345,000	$325,000

Problem 4-2 (concluded)

Requirement 2

The 2003 income from discontinued operations would include only the operating loss of $455,000.   Since no impairment loss is indicated ($7,000,000 – 6,200,000 = 800,000 anticipated gain), none is included. The anticipated gain on disposal is not recognized until it is realized, presumably in the following year.

Requirement 3

The 2003 income from discontinued operations would include the operating loss of $455,000 as well as an impairment loss of $1,200,000 ($6,200,000 book value of assets less $5,000,000 fair value).

EXERCISES

Exercise 5-1

Requirement 1

Year	Income recognized
2003	$250,000 ($400,000 - 150,000)
2004	- 0 -
2005	- 0 -
2006	- 0 -
2007	- 0 -
Total	$250,000

Requirement 2

Year	Cash Collected	Cost Recovery(37.5%)	Gross Profit(62.5%)
2003	$100,000	$ 37,500	$ 62,500
2004	75,000	28,125	46,875
2005	75,000	28,125	46,875
2006	75,000	28,125	46,875
2007	75,000	28,125	46,875
Totals	$400,000	$150,000	$250,000

Requirement 3

Year	Cash Collected	Cost Recovery	Gross Profit
2003	$100,000	$100,000	- 0 -
2004	75,000	50,000	$ 25,000
2005	75,000	- 0 -	75,000
2006	75,000	- 0 -	75,000
2007	75,000	- 0 -	75,000
Totals	$400,000	$150,000	$250,000

Exercise 5-2

Requirement 1

	2003	2004
Contract price	$2,600,000	$2,600,000
Actual costs to date	360,000	2,010,000
Estimated costs to complete	1,560,000	- 0 -
Total estimated costs	1,920,000	2,010,000
Estimated (actual) gross profit	$ 680,000	$ 590,000

Gross profit recognition:

2003: $\dfrac{\$360,000}{\$1,920,000} = 18.75\% \times \$680,000 = \textbf{\$127,500}$

2004: $\$590,000 - 127,500 = \textbf{\$462,500}$

Requirement 2

2003	$ - 0 -
2004	$590,000

Requirement 3

Balance Sheet
At December 31, 2003

Current assets:

Accounts receivable $ 110,000

Costs and profit ($487,500)* in excess
   of billings ($430,000)   57,500

---

* Costs ($360,000) + profit ($127,500)

Exercise 5-2 (concluded)

Requirement 4

Balance Sheet
At December 31, 2003

Current assets:

Accounts receivable $ 110,000

Current liabilities:

Billings ($430,000) in excess of costs ($360,000) $ 70,000

Exercise 5-3

Requirement 1

	2003	2004	2005
Contract price	$12,000,000	$12,000,000	$12,000,000
Actual costs to date	3,000,000	7,000,000	12,800,000
Estimated costs to complete	6,000,000	5,600,000	- 0 -
Total estimated costs	9,000,000	12,600,000	12,800,000
Estimated gross profit (loss)	$ 3,000,000	$ (600,000)	$ (800,000)

Gross profit (loss) recognition:

2003: $\dfrac{\$3,000,000}{\$9,000,000} = 33.3333\%$ x $3,000,000 = **$1,000,000**

2004: $(600,000) - 1,000,000   = **$(1,600,000)**

2005: $(800,000) - (600,000) = **$(200,000)**

Exercise 5-3 (continued)

Requirement 2

	2003	2004
Construction in progress	3,000,000	4,000,000
Various accounts	3,000,000	4,000,000
To record construction costs.		
Accounts receivable	3,800,000	3,500,000
Billings on construction contract	3,800,000	3,500,000
To record progress billings.		
Cash	3,250,000	3,600,000
Accounts receivable	3,250,000	3,600,000
To record cash collections.		
Construction in progress		
(gross profit)	1,000,000	
Cost of construction	3,000,000	
Revenue from long-term contracts		
(33.3333% x $12,000,000)	4,000,000	
To record gross profit.		
Cost of construction (2)		4,266,667
Revenue from long-term contracts (1)		2,666,667
Construction in progress (loss)		1,600,000
To record expected loss.		

(1) and (2):

Percent complete = $7,000,000 ÷ $12,600,000 = 55.55%

Revenue recognized to date:	
55.55% x $12,000,000 =	$6,666,667
Less: Revenue recognized in 2003 (above)	(4,000,000)
Revenue recognized in 2004	2,666,667 (1)
Plus: Loss recognized in 2004 (above)	1,600,000
Cost of construction, 2004	$4,266,667 (2)

Exercise 5-3 (concluded)

Requirement 3

Balance Sheet	2003	2004
Current assets:		
Accounts receivable	$550,000	$450,000
Costs and profit ($4,000,000)* in		
excess of billings ($3,800,000)	200,000	
Current liabilities:		
Billings ($7,300,000) in excess		
of costs less loss ($6,400,000)		$900,000

* Costs ($3,000,000) + profit ($1,000,000)

Exercise 5-4

November 15, 2003	**To record franchise agreement and down payment**	
Cash (50% x $25,000)	12,500	
Note receivable	12,500	
Unearned franchise fee revenue		25,000

February 15, 2004	**To recognize franchise fee revenue**	
Unearned franchise fee revenue......................................	25,000	
Franchise fee revenue		25,000

Exercise 5-5

Turnover ratios for Garret & Sons Music Company for 2003:

$$\text{Inventory turnover ratio} = \frac{\$6,000,000}{[\$850,000 + 700,000] \div 2}$$

$$= \underline{7.74 \text{ times}}$$

$$\text{Receivables turnover ratio} = \frac{\$10,000,000}{[\$800,000 + 600,000] \div 2}$$

$$= \underline{14.29 \text{ times}}$$

$$\text{Average collection period} = \frac{365}{14.29}$$

$$= \underline{25.5 \text{ days}}$$

$$\text{Asset turnover ratio} = \frac{\$10,000,000}{[\$4,490,000 + 4,100,000] \div 2}$$

$$= \underline{2.33 \text{ times}}$$

The company turns its inventory over 7 times per year compared to the industry average of 6 times per year. The asset turnover ratio also is slightly better than the industry average (2.33 times per year versus 2 times). These ratios indicate that Garret & Sons is able to generate more sales per dollar invested in inventory and in total assets than the industry averages. The company also is able to collect its receivables quicker than the industry average (25.5 days compared to the industry average of 28 days).

Exercise 5-6

Requirement 1

 a. **Profit margin on sales** $360 \div \$7,200 = 5\%$

 b. **Return on assets** $360 \div [(\$2,900 + 2,700) \div 2] = 12.86\%$

 c. **Return on shareholders' equity** $360 \div [(\$1,700 + 1,550) \div 2] = 22.2\%$

Requirement 2

Retained earnings beginning of period	$550,000
Add: Net income	360,000
	910,000
Less: Retained earnings end of period	700,000
Dividends paid	$210,000

PROBLEMS

Problem 5-1

Requirement 1

Total profit = $800,000 - 400,000 = $400,000

Installment sales method: Gross profit % = $400,000 ÷ $800,000 = 50%

	10/31/03	10/31/04	10/31/05	10/31/06
Cash collections	$200,000	$200,000	$200,000	$200,000
a. Point of delivery method	$400,000	- 0 -	- 0 -	- 0 -
b. Installment sales method (50% x cash collected)	$100,000	$100,000	$100,000	$100,000
c. Cost recovery method	- 0 -	- 0 -	$200,000	$200,000

Problem 5-1 (continued)

Requirement 2

	Point of Delivery		Installment Sales		Cost Recovery	
Installment receivable	800,000					
Sales revenue		800,000				
Cost of goods sold	400,000					
Inventory		400,000				
To record sale on 10/31/03.						
Installment receivable			800,000		800,000	
Inventory				400,000		400,000
Deferred gross profit				400,000		400,000
To record sale on 10/31/03.						
Cash	200,000		200,000		200,000	
Installment receivable		200,000		200,000		200,000
Entry made each Oct. 31.						
Deferred gross profit			100,000			
Realized gross profit				100,000		
To record gross profit.						
(entry made each Oct. 31)						
Deferred gross profit					200,000	
Realized gross profit						200,000
To record gross profit.						
(entry made 10/31/05 & 10/31/06)						

Problem 5-1 (concluded)

Requirement 3

	Point of Delivery	Installment Sales	Cost Recovery
December 31, 2003			
Assets			
Installment receivable	600,000	600,000	600,000
Liabilities			
Deferred gross profit from installment sale	- 0 -	300,000	400,000
December 31, 2004			
Assets			
Installment receivable	400,000	400,000	400,000
Liabilities			
Deferred gross profit from installment sale		200,000	400,000

Problem 5-2

Requirement 1

	2003	2004	2005
Contract price	$15,000,000	$15,000,000	$15,000,000
Actual costs to date	4,000,000	8,800,000	13,000,000
Estimated costs to complete	8,000,000	4,000,000	- 0 -
Total estimated costs	12,000,000	12,800,000	13,000,000
Estimated gross profit (loss)	$ 3,000,000	$ 2,200,000	$ 2,000,000

Gross profit (loss) recognition:

2003: $\dfrac{\$4,000,000}{\$12,000,000} = 33.33\% \times \$3,000,000 = \mathbf{\$1,000,000}$

2004: $\dfrac{\$8,800,000}{\$12,800,000} = 68.75\% \times \$2,200,000 = \$1,512,500 - 1,000,000 = \mathbf{\$512,500}$

2005: $\$2,000,000 - 1,512,500 = \mathbf{\$487,500}$

Requirement 2

	2003	2004	2005
Construction in progress	4,000,000	4,800,000	4,200,000
Various accounts	4,000,000	4,800,000	4,200,000
To record construction costs.			
Accounts receivable	3,500,000	5,000,000	6,500,000
Billings on construction contract	3,500,000	5,000,000	6,500,000
To record progress billings.			
Cash	2,800,000	5,600,000	6,600,000
Accounts receivable	2,800,000	5,600,000	6,600,000
To record cash collections.			
Construction in progress (gross profit)	1,000,000	512,500	487,500
Cost of construction (cost incurred)	4,000,000	4,800,000	4,200,000
Revenue from long-term contracts(1)	5,000,000	5,312,500	4,687,500
To record gross profit.			

Problem 5-2 *(continued)*

(1) Revenue recognized:

2003: 33.33% x $15,000,000	=		<u>$5,000,000</u>
2004: 68.75% x $15,000,000	=	$10,312,500	
Less: Revenue recognized in 2003		(5,000,000)	
Revenue recognized in 2004			<u>$5,312,500</u>
2005: 100% x $15,000,000	=	$15,000,000	
Less: Revenue recognized in 2003 & 2004		(10,312,500)	
Revenue recognized in 2005			<u>$4,687,500</u>

Requirement 3

Balance Sheet		**2003**		**2004**
Current assets:				
Accounts receivable		$ 700,000		$100,000
Construction in progress	$5,000,000		$10,312,500	
Less: Billings	(3,500,000)		(8,500,000)	
Costs and profit in excess				
of billings		1,500,000		1,812,500

Requirement 4

	2003	**2004**	**2005**
Costs incurred during the year	$4,000,000	$4,200,000	$7,200,000
Estimated costs to complete			
as of year-end	8,000,000	7,100,000	-

	2003	**2004**	**2005**
Contract price	<u>$15,000,000</u>	<u>$15,000,000</u>	<u>$15,000,000</u>
Actual costs to date	4,000,000	8,200,000	15,400,000
Estimated costs to complete	8,000,000	7,100,000	- 0 -
Total estimated costs	12,000,000	15,300,000	15,400,000
Estimated gross profit (loss)	$ 3,000,000	$ (300,000)	$ (400,000)

Problem 5-2 (concluded)

Gross profit (loss) recognition:

2003: $\dfrac{\$4,000,000}{\$12,000,000} = 33.33\% \times \$3,000,000 = \mathbf{\$1,000,000}$

2004: $100\% \times \$(300,000) = \$(300,000) - 1,000,000 = \mathbf{\$(1,300,000)}$

2005: $\$(400,000) - (300,000) = \mathbf{\$(100,000)}$

Chapter 6 Time Value of Money Concepts

EXERCISES

Exercise 6-1

1. FV = $50,000 x 2.15892* = $107,946

* Future value of $1: n=10, i=8% (from Table 6A-1)

2. FV = $30,000 x 3.20714* = $96,214

* Future value of $1: n=20, i=6% (from Table 6A-1)

3. FV = $40,000 x 17.44940* = $697,976

* Future value of $1: n=30, i=10% (from Table 6A-1)

4. FV = $60,000 x 1.60103* = $96,062

* Future value of $1: n=12, i=4% (from Table 6A-1)

Exercise 6-2

1. PV = $20,000 x .46319* = $9,264

* Present value of $1: n=10, i=8% (from Table 6A-2)

2. PV = $10,000 x .31180* = $3,118

* Present value of $1: n=20, i=6% (from Table 6A-2)

3. PV = $25,000 x .05731* = $1,433

* Present value of $1: n=30, i=10% (from Table 6A-2)

4. PV = $40,000 x .40388* = $16,155

* Present value of $1: n=8, i=12% (from Table 6A-2)

Exercise 6-3

1. PVA = $10,000 x 3.79079* = $37,908

* Present value of an ordinary annuity of $1: n=5, i=10% (from Table 6A-4)

2. PVAD = $10,000 x 4.16986* = $41,699

* Present value of an annuity due of $1: n=5, i=10% (from Table 6A-6)

Exercise 6-4

1. PV = $50,000 x .46319* = $23,160

* Present value of $1: n=10, i=8% (from Table 6A-2)

2. $\dfrac{\$31,947}{\$70,000}$ = .45639*

* Present value of $1: n=20, i=**?** (from Table 6A-2, i = approximately **4%**)

3. $\dfrac{\$\ 9,576}{\$40,000}$ = .2394*

* Present value of $1: n=**?**, i=10% (from Table 6A-2, n = approximately **15 years**)

4. $\dfrac{\$\ 20,462}{\$100,000}$ = .20462*

* Present value of $1: n=14, i=**?** (from Table 6A-2, i = approximately **12%**)

5. FV = $15,000 x 5.74349* = $86,152

* Future value of $1: n=30, i=6% (from Table 6A-1)

Exercise 6-5

1. PVA = $5,000 x 6.14457* = $30,723

    * Present value of an ordinary annuity of $1: n=10, i=10% (from Table 6A-4)

2. $\dfrac{\$298,058}{\$60,000}$ = 4.96764*

    * Present value of an ordinary annuity of $1: n=8, i=? (from Table 6A-4, i = approximately **12%**)

3. $\dfrac{\$337,733}{\$30,000}$ = 11.25777*

    * Present value of an ordinary annuity of $1: n=?, i= 8% (from Table 6A-4, n = approximately **30 years**)

4. $\dfrac{\$600,000}{\$74,435}$ = 8.06072*

    * Present value of an ordinary annuity of $1: n=15, i=? (from Table 6A-4, i = approximately **9%**)

5. $\dfrac{\$200,000}{4.11141^*}$ = $48,645

    * Present value of an ordinary annuity of $1: n=6, i=12% (from Table 6A-4)

Exercise 6-6

PV = ? x .80426* = $4,800

PV = $\dfrac{\$4,800}{.80426^*}$ = $5,968

* Present value of $1: n=11, i=2% (from Table 6A-2)

PVA = $\underset{\text{annuity amount}}{?}$ x 14.99203* = $5,968

PVA = $\dfrac{\$5,968}{14.99203^*}$ = $398.08 = Payment

* Present value of an ordinary annuity of $1: n=18, i=2% (from Table 6A-4)

PROBLEMS

Problem 6-1

1. $PV = \$50{,}000 + (\$20{,}000 \times 3.31213^*) = \$116{,}243 = $ Equipment

* Present value of an ordinary annuity of $1: n=4, i=8% (from Table 6A-4)

2. $\$600{,}000 = $ Annuity amount $\times 4.24646^*$

* Future value of an ordinary annuity of $1: n=4, i=4% (from Table 6A-3)

$$\text{Annuity amount} = \frac{\$600{,}000}{4.24646}$$

Annuity amount $= \$141{,}294 = $ Required annual deposit

3. Choose the option with the lowest present value of cash outflows.

1. *Buy option:*

$PV = -\$2{,}000{,}000$

2. *Lease option:*

$PVAD = -\$200{,}000 \times 9.36492^* = -\$1{,}872{,}984$

* Present value of an annuity due of $1: n=10, i=10% (from Table 6A-6)

Reuter should **lease** the machine.

Problem 6-2

Choose the alternative with the highest present value.

Alternative 1:

PV = $400,000

Alternative 2:

PV = PVAD = $40,000 x 10.29498* = **$411,799**

* Present value of an annuity due of $1: n=15, i=6% (from Table 6A-6)

Alternative 3:

PVA = $45,000   x   9.71225*   = $437,051

* Present value of an ordinary annuity of $1: n=15, i=6% (from Table 6A-4)

PV   = $437,051   x   .79209*   = $346,184

* Present value of $1: n=4, i=6% (from Table 6A-2)

Smokey should choose alternative **2**.

EXERCISES

Exercise 7-1

Requirement 1

Sales price = 200 units x \$800 = \$160,000 x 80% = *\$128,000*

April 6, 2003
Accounts receivable 128,000
    Sales revenue   128,000

April 16, 2003
Cash (99% x \$128,000) 126,720
Sales discounts (1% x \$128,000) 1,280
    Accounts receivable   128,000

Requirement 2

April 6, 2003
Accounts receivable 128,000
    Sales revenue   128,000

May 6, 2003
Cash.. 128,000
    Accounts receivable   128,000

Exercise 7-1 (concluded)

Requirement 3

Requirement 1:

April 6, 2003		
Accounts receivable	126,720	
Sales revenue (99% x $128,000)		126,720

April 16, 2003		
Cash..	126,720	
Accounts receivable		126,720

Requirement 2:

April 6, 2003		
Accounts receivable	126,720	
Sales revenue (99% x $128,000)		126,720

May 6, 2003		
Cash..	128,000	
Accounts receivable		126,720
Interest revenue		1,280

Exercise 7-2

Requirement 1

To record the write-off of receivables.

Allowance for uncollectible accounts 46,200

    Accounts receivable   46,200

Allowance for uncollectible accounts:

Balance, beginning of year	$68,000
Deduct: Receivables written off	(46,200)
Balance, before adjusting entry for 2003 bad debts	21,800
Required allowance: 3% x $2,223,000	(66,690)
Bad debt expense	$44,890

To record bad debt expense for the year.

Bad debt expense 44,890

    Allowance for uncollectible accounts........................   44,890

Requirement 2

Current assets:

Accounts receivable, net of $66,690 in allowance for uncollectible accounts	$2,156,310

Exercise 7-3

Requirement 1

March 31, 2003

Note receivable (face amount)...	80,000	
Discount on note receivable ($80,000 x 6%)................		4,800
Sales revenue (difference)		75,200

December 31, 2003

Discount on note receivable	3,600	
Interest revenue ($80,000 x 6% x $9/12$)..........................		3,600

March 31, 2004

Discount on note receivable	1,200	
Interest revenue ($80,000 x 6% x $3/12$)..........................		1,200

Cash	80,000	
Note receivable (face amount).......................................		80,000

Requirement 2

     $ 4,800   interest for 12 months
   ÷ $75,200   sales price
   = 6.38%   = effective interest rate

Exercise 7-4

Cash (difference)	90,000	
Loss on sale of receivables (1% x $100,000)	1,000	
Receivable from factor ([10% x $100,000] – $1,000 fee)	9,000	
Accounts receivable (balance sold)..............................		100,000

Exercise 7-5

Cash (difference)	90,000	
Loss on sale of receivables ([1% x $100,000] + $4,000)	5,000	
Receivable from factor ([10% x $100,000] – $1,000 fee)	9,000	
Recourse liability		4,000
Accounts receivable (balance sold)................................		100,000

Exercise 7-6

Step 1: Accrue interest earned.

September 1, 2003

Interest receivable	1,000	
Interest revenue ($50,000 x 8% x $^{3}/_{12}$).........................		1,000

Step 2: Add interest to maturity to calculate maturity value.
Step 3: Deduct discount to calculate cash proceeds.

$50,000	Face amount
4,000	Interest to maturity ($50,000 x 8%)
54,000	*Maturity value*
(4,050)	Discount ($54,000 x 10% x $^{9}/_{12}$)
$49,950	*Cash proceeds*

Step 4: To record a loss for the difference between the cash proceeds and the note's book value.

September 1, 2003

Cash (proceeds determined above)	49,950	
Loss on sale of note receivable (difference)......................	1,050	
Note receivable (face amount).......................................		50,000
Interest receivable (accrued interest determined above).....		1,000

Exercise 7-7

Requirement 1

> ### Step 1:   Bank Balance to Corrected Balance
>
> | | |
> |---|---|
> | *Balance per bank statement* | $74,674 |
> | Add: Deposits outstanding | 8,200 |
> | Deduct: Checks outstanding | (8,420) |
> | Corrected cash balance | $74,454 |
>
> ### Step 2:   Book Balance to Corrected Balance
>
> | | |
> |---|---|
> | *Balance per books* | $78,984 |
> | Deduct: | |
> | Service charges | (50) |
> | NSF checks | (680) |
> | Automatic monthly transfer | (2,000) |
> | Error in recording cash disbursement | |
> | ($2,000 – 200) | (1,800) |
> | Corrected cash balance | $74,454 |

Requirement 2

To record credits to cash revealed by the bank reconciliation.

Miscellaneous expense (bank service charges)	50	
Accounts receivable (NSF checks)	680	
Cash - savings account	2,000	
Accounts payable	1,800	
Cash		4,530

Note: Each of the adjustments to the book balance required journal entries.
None of the adjustments to the bank balance require entries.

PROBLEMS

Problem 7-1

Requirement 1

Monthly bad debt expense accrual summary.

Bad debt expense (2% x $3,800,000).................................	76,000	
Allowance for uncollectible accounts.........................		76,000

To record year 2003 accounts receivable write-offs.

Allowance for uncollectible accounts :...........................	82,000	
Accounts receivable		82,000

Requirement 2

Bad debt expense	4,700	
Allowance for uncollectible accounts **(below)**.............		4,700

Year-end required allowance for uncollectible accounts:

Summary			
Age Group	**Amount**	**Percent Uncollectible**	**Estimated Allowance**
0-60 days	$ 825,000	2%	$ 16,500
61-90 days	220,000	10%	22,000
91-120 days	50,000	30%	15,000
Over 120 days	128,000	40%	51,200
Totals	$1,223,000		$104,700

Problem 7-1 (concluded)

Allowance for uncollectible accounts:

Beginning balance	$106,000
Add: Monthly bad debt accruals	76,000
Deduct: Write-offs	(82,000)
Balance before year-end adjustment	100,000
Required allowance (determined above)	104,700
Required year-end increase in allowance	$ 4,700

Requirement 3

Bad debt expense for 2003:

Monthly accruals	$76,000
Year-end adjustment	4,700
Total	$80,700

Balance sheet:

Current assets:
  Accounts receivable, net of $104,700 in
    allowance for uncollectible accounts $1,118,300

Problem 7-2

Requirement 1

March 31, 2003

Note receivable (face amount)	12,000	
Discount ($12,000 x 10%)		1,200
Sales revenue (difference)		10,800

April 12, 2003

Accounts receivable	10,000	
Sales revenue		10,000

April 21, 2003

Cash (98% x $10,000)	9,800	
Sales discounts (2% x $10,000)	200	
Accounts receivable		10,000

April 27, 2003

Sales returns	8,000	
Accounts receivable		8,000
Inventory	6,000	
Cost of goods sold		6,000

Problem 7-2 (continued)

May 30, 2003
Cash (98% x $100,000)... 98,000
Loss on sale of receivables (2% x $100,000) 2,000
    Accounts receivable 100,000

July 31, 2003
Note receivable 15,000
    Sales revenue 15,000

To accrue interest on note receivable for two months.

Sept. 30, 2003
Interest receivable 200
    Interest revenue ($15,000 x 8% x $^2/_{12}$)......................... 200

To record discounting of note receivable.

Sept. 30, 2003
Cash (proceeds determined below) 14,976
Loss on sale of note receivable (difference)..................... 224
    Interest receivable (from adjusting entry)....................... 200
    Note receivable (face amount) 15,000

Problem 7-2 (concluded)

$15,000	Face amount
600	Interest to maturity ($15,000 x 8% x $6/12$)
15,600	*Maturity value*
(624)	Discount ($15,600 x 12% x $4/12$)
$14,976	*Cash proceeds*

Requirement 2

To accrue nine months' interest on the Misthos Co. note receivable.

Discount	900	
Interest revenue ($12,000 x 10% x $9/12$)........................		900

Chapter 8 Inventories: Measurement

EXERCISES
Exercise 8-1

PERPETUAL SYSTEM		PERIODIC SYSTEM	
	($ in 000s)		
Purchases			
Inventory	265	Purchases	265
Accounts payable	265	Accounts payable	265
Freight			
Inventory	16	Freight-in	16
Accounts payable	16	Accounts payable	16
Returns			
Accounts payable	6	Accounts payable	6
Inventory	6	Purchase returns	6
Sales			
Accounts receivable	350	Accounts receivable	350
Sales revenue	350	Sales revenue	350
Cost of goods sold	264	No entry	
Inventory	264		
End of period			
No entry		Cost of goods sold (below)	264
		Inventory (ending)	123
		Purchase returns	6
		Inventory (beginning)	112
		Purchases	265
		Freight-in	16

Cost of goods sold:		
Beginning inventory		$112
Purchases	$265	
Less: Returns	(6)	
Plus: Freight-in	16	
Net purchases		275
Cost of goods available		387
Less: Ending inventory		(123)
Cost of goods sold		$264

Exercise 8-2

Requirement 1

Purchase price = 50 units x $800 = $40,000 x .75 = $30,000

January 14, 2003

Purchases 30,000

    Accounts payable   30,000

January 23, 2003

Accounts payable 30,000

    Purchase discounts (2% x $30,000)   600

    Cash (98% x $30,000)   29,400

Requirement 2

January 14, 2003

Purchases 30,000

    Accounts payable   30,000

February 13, 2003

Accounts payable 30,000

    Cash   30,000

Exercise 8-2 (concluded)

Requirement 3

Requirement 1:

January 14, 2003		
Purchases (98% x $30,000)	29,400	
Accounts payable		29,400

January 23, 2003		
Accounts payable	29,400	
Cash		29,400

Requirement 2:

January 14, 2003		
Purchases (98% x $30,000)	29,400	
Accounts payable		29,400

February 13, 2003		
Accounts payable	29,400	
Interest expense (2% x $30,000).......................................	600	
Cash		30,000

Exercise 8-3

Inventory balance before additional transactions	$317,000
Add:	
Materials purchased f.o.b. shipping point on 12/28	32,000
Deduct:	
Merchandise held on consignment from the Harvey Company	(12,000)
Correct inventory balance	$337,000

Exercise 8-4

First-in, first-out (FIFO)

Cost of goods sold:

Date of sale	Units sold	Cost of Units Sold	Total Cost
March 14	3,000 (from BI)	$8.00	$24,000
	1,000 (from 3/8 purchase)	8.40	8,400
March 25	4,000 (from 3/8 purchase)	8.40	33,600
	3,000 (from 3/18 purchase)	8.20	24,600
Total	11,000		$90,600

Ending inventory = 3,000 units x $8.20 = $24,600

Exercise 8-4 (continued)

Last-in, first-out (LIFO)

Date	Purchased			Sold		Balance	
Beginning inventory	3,000 @ $8.00	=	$24,000			3,000 @ $8.00	$24,000
March 8	5,000 @ $8.40	=	$42,000			3,000 @ $8.00 5,000 @ $8.40	$66,000
March 14				4,000 @ $ 8.40 =	$33,600	3,000 @ $8.00 1,000 @ $8.40	$32,400
March 18	6,000 @ $8.20	=	$49,200			3,000 @ $8.00 1,000 @ $8.40 6,000 @ $8.20	$81,600
March 25				6,000 @ $8.20 = 1,000 @ $8.40 =	$49,200 $ 8,400	3,000 @ $8.00	**$24,000** *Ending inventory*
			Total cost of goods sold	=	**$91,200**		

Exercise 8-4 (concluded)

Average cost

Date	Purchased	Sold	Balance	
Beginning inventory	3,000 @ $8.00 = $24,000		3,000 @ $8.00	$24,000
March 8	5,000 @ $8.40 = $42,000 $\dfrac{\$66,000}{8,000 \text{ units}}$ = $8.25/unit			
March 14		4,000 @ $8.25 = $33,000	4,000 @ $8.25	$33,000
March 18	6,000 @ $8.20 = $49,200 $\dfrac{\$82,200}{10,000 \text{ units}}$ = $8.22/unit			
March 25		7,000 @ $8.22 = $57,540	3,000 @ $8.22	**$24,660** *Ending inventory*
	Total cost of goods sold	= **$90,540**		

Exercise 8-5

Requirement 1

Cost of goods available for sale:

Beginning inventory (7,000 x $22.00)		$154,000
Purchases:		
6,000 x $22.65	$135,900	
9,000 x $24.00	216,000	351,900
Cost of goods available (22,000 units)		$505,900

Cost of goods available for sale (22,000 units)	$505,900
Less: Ending inventory (below)	(207,000)
Cost of goods sold	$298,900

Cost of ending inventory:

$$\text{Weighted-average unit cost} = \frac{\$505,900}{22,000 \text{ units}} = \$23 \text{ (rounded)}$$

9,000 units x $23 (rounded) = $207,000

Exercise 8-5 (concluded)

Requirement 2

Date	Purchased	Sold	Balance	
Beginning inventory	7,000 @ $22.00 = $154,000		7,000 @ $22.00	$154,000
April 5	6,000 @ $22.65 = $135,900 $$\frac{\$289,900}{13,000 \text{ units}} = \$22.30/\text{unit}$$			
April 11		5,000 @ $22.30 = $111,500	8,000 @ $22.20	$178,400
April 26	9,000 @ $24.00 = $216,000 $$\frac{\$394,400}{17,000 \text{ units}} = \$23.20/\text{unit}$$			
April 28		8,000 @ $23.20 = $185,600	9,000 @ $23.20	$208,800 *Ending inventory*
	Total cost of goods sold	= $297,100		

Exercise 8-6

Date	Ending Inventory at Base Year Cost	Inventory Layers at Base Year Cost	Inventory Layers Converted to Cost	Ending Inventory DVL Cost
1/1/03	$\dfrac{\$832,000}{1.00} = \$832,000$	$832,000 (base)	$832,000 x 1.00 = $832,000	$832,000
12/31/03	$\dfrac{\$954,000}{1.02} = \$935,294$	$832,000 (base) 103,294 (2003)	$832,000 x 1.00 = $832,000 103,294 x 1.02 = 105,360	**937,360**
12/31/04	$\dfrac{\$975,000}{1.05} = \$928,571$	$832,000 (base) 96,571 (2003)	$832,000 x 1.00 = $832,000 96,571 x 1.02 = 98,502	**930,502**

PROBLEMS

Problem 8-1

Requirement 1

Beginning inventory (8,000 x $10.00)		$ 80,000
Net purchases:		
Purchases (45,000* units x $12.00)	$540,000	
Less: Purchase discounts		
($11 x 40,000 units x 80% x 2%)	(7,040)	532,960
Cost of goods available (53,000 units)		612,960
Less: Ending inventory (below)		(70,000)
Cost of goods sold		$542,960

* The 5,000 units purchased on December 28 are included. The units were shipped f.o.b. shipping point before year-end. The $12 unit cost includes freight charges.

Cost of ending inventory:

Date of purchase	Units	Unit cost	Total cost
BI	7,000	$ 10.00	$ 70,000

Problem 8-2

Cost of goods available for sale for periodic system:

Beginning inventory (10,000 x $25.00)		$250,000
Purchases:		
8,000 x $24.00	$192,000	
7,000 x $27.00	189,000	381,000
Cost of goods available (25,000 units)		$631,000

1. FIFO, periodic system

Cost of goods available for sale (25,000 units)	$631,000
Less: Ending inventory (determined below)	(309,000)
Cost of goods sold	$322,000

Cost of ending inventory:

Date of purchase	Units	Unit cost	Total cost
Jan. 22	7,000	$27.00	$189,000
Jan. 4	5,000	24.00	120,000
Totals	12,000		$309,000

2. LIFO, periodic system

Cost of goods available for sale (25,000 units)	$631,000
Less: Ending inventory (determined below)	(298,000)
Cost of goods sold	$333,000

Cost of ending inventory:

Date of purchase	Units	Unit cost	Total cost
BI	10,000	$25.00	$250,000
Jan. 4	2,000	24.00	48,000
Totals	12,000		$298,000

Problem 8-2 (concluded)

3. Average cost, periodic system

Cost of goods available for sale (25,000 units) $631,000
  Less: Ending inventory (below)   (302,880)
   Cost of goods sold $328,120*

Cost of ending inventory:

$$\text{Weighted-average unit cost} \ = \ \frac{\$631,000}{25,000 \text{ units}} \ = \ \$25.24$$

12,000 units x $25.24 = $302,880

* Alternatively, could be determined by multiplying the units sold by the average cost: 13,000 units x $25.24 = $328,120

EXERCISES

Exercise 9-1

Requirement 1

Product	(1) RC	(2) Ceiling NRV	(3) Floor NRV-NP (NP= 20% of cost)	(4) Designated Market Value [Middle value of (1)-(3)]	(5) Cost	Inventory Value [Lower of (4) or (5)]
Gloves	$330,000	$300,000	$228,000	$300,000	$360,000	$300,000
Bats	240,000	320,000	268,000	268,000	260,000	260,000
Balls	110,000	125,000	95,000	110,000	150,000	110,000
Uniforms	560,000	950,000	830,000	830,000	600,000	600,000
				Totals	$1,370,000	$1,270,000

The inventory value is **$1,270,000**.

Requirement 2

Loss from write-down of inventory: $1,370,000 - 1,270,000 = **$100,000**

Exercise 9-2

Merchandise inventory, January 1, 2003		$ 4,500,000
Purchases		14,500,000
Freight-in		1,000,000
Cost of goods available for sale		20,000,000
Less: Cost of goods sold:		
Sales	$23,000,000	
Less: Estimated gross profit of 40%	(9,200,000)	(13,800,000)
Estimated loss from fire		$ 6,200,000

Exercise 9-3

	Cost	Retail
Beginning inventory	$40,000	$60,000
Plus: Net purchases	28,250	37,000
Net markups		2,000
Less: Net markdowns		(1,500)
Goods available for sale	68,250	97,500

Cost-to-retail percentage: $\dfrac{\$68{,}250}{\$97{,}500} = 70\%$

Less: Net sales		(45,000)
Estimated ending inventory at retail		$52,500
Estimated ending inventory at cost (70% x $52,500)	(36,750)	
Estimated cost of goods sold	$31,500	

Exercise 9-4

	Cost	Retail
Beginning inventory	$ 180,000	$ 300,000
Plus: Purchases	1,479,000	2,430,000
Freight-in	30,000	
Less: Purchase returns	(60,000)	(105,000)
Plus: Net markups		90,000
		2,715,000

Cost-to-retail percentage: $\dfrac{\$1,629,000}{\$2,715,000} = 60\%$

	Cost	Retail
Less: Net markdowns		(45,000)
Goods available for sale	1,629,000	2,670,000
Less:		
Normal spoilage		(63,000)
Net sales		(2,340,000)
Estimated ending inventory at retail		$ 267,000
Estimated ending inventory at cost (60% x $267,000)	(160,200)	
Estimated cost of goods sold	$1,468,800	

Exercise 9-5

	Cost	Retail
Beginning inventory	$213,840	$ 396,000
Plus: Net purchases	360,000	765,000
Net markups		18,000
Less: Net markdowns		(33,000)
Goods available for sale (excluding beginning inventory)	360,000	750,000
Goods available for sale (including beginning inventory)	573,840	1,146,000

Base year cost-to-retail percentage: $\dfrac{\$213,840}{\$396,000} = 54\%$

2003 cost-to-retail percentage: $\dfrac{\$360,000}{\$750,000} = 48\%$

		Retail
Less: Net sales		(690,000)
Estimated ending inventory at current year retail prices		$456,000

	Cost
Estimated ending inventory at cost (below)	(238,838)
Estimated cost of goods sold	$335,002

Ending Inventory at Year-end Retail Prices	Step 1 Ending Inventory at Base Year Retail Prices	Step 2 Inventory Layers at Base Year Retail Prices	Step 3 Inventory Layers Converted to Cost	
$456,000 (above)	$\dfrac{\$456,000}{1.02} = \$447,059$	$396,000 (base) 51,059 (2003)	x 1.00 x 54% = x 1.02 x 48% =	$213,840 24,998

Total ending inventory at dollar-value LIFO retail cost **$238,838**

Exercise 9-6

1. To increase inventory by $1.6 million and increase retained earnings to what it would have been if 2002 cost of goods sold had been calculated correctly.

```
Analysis:
        2002                                    2003
     Beginning inventory              Beginning inventory      U
     Purchases                        Purchases
     Less: Ending inventory     U
     Cost of goods sold         O

     Revenues
     Less: Cost of goods sold   O
     Less: Other expenses                     U = Understated
     Net income                 U             O = Overstated
          ↓
     Retained earnings          U
                                              ($ in millions)
  Inventory ...................................        1.6
      Retained earnings ........................           1.6
```

2. The 2002 financial statements that were incorrect as a result of the error would be *retroactively restated* to reflect the correct cost of goods sold, (income tax expense if taxes are considered), net income, ending inventory, and retained earnings when those statements are reported again for comparative purposes in the 2003 annual report.

3. Because retained earnings is one of the accounts incorrect, the correction to that account is reported as a *prior period adjustment* to the 2002 retained earnings balance in the comparative statements of shareholders' equity.

4. Also, a *disclosure note* should describe the nature of the error and the impact of its correction on each year's net income, income before extraordinary items, and earnings per share.

PROBLEMS

Problem 9-1

1. Average cost

	Cost	Retail
Beginning inventory	$140,000	$280,000
Plus: Purchases	420,000	690,000
Freight-in	16,000	
Less: Purchase returns	(12,000)	(18,000)
Plus: Net markups		24,000
Less: Net markdowns		(26,000)
Abnormal spoilage		(10,000)
Goods available for sale	564,000	940,000

Cost-to-retail percentage: $\dfrac{\$564,000}{\$940,000} = 60\%$

Less:		
Normal spoilage		(5,000)
Sales:		
Net sales ($700,000 - 20,000)	$680,000	
Add back employee discounts	6,000	(686,000)
Estimated ending inventory at retail		$249,000
Estimated ending inventory at cost (60% x $249,000)	(149,400)	
Estimated cost of goods sold	$414,600	

Problem 9-1 (concluded)

2. Conventional (average, LCM)

	Cost	Retail
Beginning inventory	$140,000	$280,000
Plus: Purchases	420,000	690,000
Freight-in	16,000	
Less: Purchase returns	(12,000)	(18,000)
Plus: Net markups		24,000
Less: Abnormal spoilage		(10,000)
		966,000

Cost-to-retail percentage: $\dfrac{\$564,000}{\$966,000} = 58.39\%$

	Cost	Retail
Less: Net markdowns		(26,000)
Goods available for sale	564,000	940,000
Normal spoilage		(5,000)
Sales:		
Net sales ($700,000 - 20,000) $680,000		
Add back employee discounts 6,000		(686,000)
Estimated ending inventory at retail		$249,000
Estimated ending inventory at cost (58.39% x $249,000)	(145,391)	
Estimated cost of goods sold	$418,609	

Problem 9-2

($ in 000s)	Cost	Retail
	Cost	**Retail**
Beginning inventory	$ 128	$ 200
Plus: Net purchases	1,072	1,600
Freight-in	59	
Net markups		6
Less: Purchase returns	(2)	(3)
Net markdowns		(13)
Goods available for sale (excluding beginning inventory)	1,129	1,590
Goods available for sale (including beginning inventory)	1,257	1,790

Base layer cost-to-retail percentage: $\dfrac{\$128}{\$200} = 64\%$

2003 layer cost-to-retail percentage: $\dfrac{\$1,129}{\$1,590} = 71\%$

	Retail
Less: Net sales	(1,465)
Estimated ending inventory at current year retail prices	$ 325

	Cost
Estimated ending inventory at cost (calculated below)	(205)
Estimated cost of goods sold	$1,052

Ending Inventory at Year-end Retail Prices	Step 1 Ending Inventory at Base Year Retail Prices	Step 2 Inventory Layers at Base Year Retail Prices	Step 3 Inventory Layers Converted to Cost	
$325 (above)	$\dfrac{\$325}{1.08} = \$301$	$200 (base) 101 (2003)	x 1.00 x 64% = x 1.08 x 71% =	$128 77
Total ending inventory at dollar-value LIFO retail cost				**$205**

EXERCISES

Exercise 10-1
Calculation of goodwill:

Purchase price		$25,000,000
Less *fair* value of net assets:		
Book value of net assets	$16,250,000	
Plus: Fair value in excess of book value:		
Property, plant, and equipment	1,000,000	
Intangible assets	2,970,000	
Less: Book value in excess of fair value:		
Receivables	(150,000)	20,070,000
Goodwill		$ 4,930,000

Exercise 10-2

Requirement 1

Machine ($25,000 cash + $46,229 present value of note)	71,229	
Cash..		25,000
Note payable (determined below)		46,229

Present value of note payments:

$$PV = \$10,000 \ (4.62288^*) = \$46,229$$

* Present value of an ordinary annuity of $1: $n=6$, $i=8\%$ (from Table 6A-4)

Requirement 2

Interest expense ($46,229 x 8%).......................................	3,698	
Note payable (difference)..	6,302	
Cash..		10,000

Requirement 3

Interest expense [($46,229 - 6,302) x 8%].........................	3,194	
Note payable (difference)..	6,806	
Cash..		10,000

Exercise 10-3

Truck - new ($800 + 14,000)	14,800	
Accumulated depreciation (balance)	12,000	
Loss ($1,000 - 800)	200	
Cash..		14,000
Truck - old (balance)		13,000

This is an exchange of similar assets and no monetary consideration is received. The loss indicated (book value of old equipment less fair value) *is* recognized. The new equipment is valued at the fair value of the old equipment ($800) plus the cash given ($14,000).

Exercise 10-4

Truck - new ($1,000 + 14,000)	15,000	
Accumulated depreciation (balance)	12,000	
Cash..		14,000
Truck - old (balance)		13,000

This is an exchange of similar assets and no monetary consideration is received. The gain indicated of $500 (fair value of old equipment less book value) *is not* recognized. The new equipment is valued at the book value of the old equipment ($1,000) plus the cash given ($14,000).

Exercise 10-5

Research and development expense:

Salaries and wages for lab research	$ 350,000
Materials used in R&D projects	400,000
Equipment	85,000
Fees paid to outsiders for R&D projects	465,000
Total	$1,300,000

The patent filing and legal costs are capitalized as the cost of the patent. The in-process research and development costs are shown as a separate line item on the income statement, if material.

Exercise 10-6

Requirement 1

	($ in millions)
Research and development expense...............................	6
Software development costs	4
Cash..	10

Requirement 2

(1) *Percentage-of-revenue method:*

$$\frac{\$5,000,000}{\$20,000,000} = 25\% \times \$4,000,000 = \$1,000,000$$

(2) *Straight-line method:*

1/3 or 33.33 % x $4,000,000 = $1,333,333

The straight-line method is used since it produces the greater amortization, **$1,333,333**.

Requirement 3

Software development costs	$4,000,000
Less: Amortization to date	(1,333,333)
Net	$2,666,667

PROBLEMS

Problem 10-1

Requirement 1
Brown:

Cash...	15,000	
New asset ($125,000 - 15,000)	110,000	
Accumulated depreciation - old asset (balance)	200,000	
Old asset (balance)		300,000
Gain on exchange of assets (below)		25,000

This is an exchange of dissimilar assets and a gain is indicated.   The entire $25,000 indicated gain ($125,000 fair value of old asset - $100,000 book value) *is* recognized. The new asset is valued at the fair value of the old asset ($125,000) less the cash received ($15,000).

Filzinger:

New asset ($110,000 + 15,000)	125,000	
Accumulated depreciation - old asset (balance)	220,000	
Cash...		15,000
Old asset (balance)		278,000
Gain on exchange of assets (below)		52,000

This is an exchange of dissimilar assets and a gain is indicated. The gain of $52,000 ($110,000 fair value of old asset - $58,000 book value) *is* recognized. The new asset is valued at the market value of the old asset ($110,000) plus the cash given ($15,000).

Problem 10-1 (continued)

Requirement 2
Brown:

Cash...	15,000	
New asset (below)	88,000	
Accumulated depreciation - old asset (balance)	200,000	
Old asset (balance)		300,000
Gain on exchange of assets (below)		3,000

This is an exchange of similar assets, a gain is indicated, and monetary consideration is received. A portion of the $25,000 indicated gain ($125,000 - $100,000) is recognized.

$$\frac{\text{Cash received}}{\text{Cash received} + \text{Fair value of similar asset received}}$$

$$\frac{\$15,000}{\$15,000 + \$110,000} = 12\%$$

Problem 10-1 (concluded)

Calculation of the Gain:

Determine Relative Fair Values of Assets Received:	Fair Values	Relative Proportions
Cash	$ 15,000	12%
New asset	110,000	88%
Total	$125,000	100%

Determine Portion of Old Asset Sold:

Portion sold (12% x $100,000)............................	$ 12,000
Portion traded (88% x $100,000)	88,000
Total book value ($300,000 – 200,000)..............	$100,000

Determine Gain on Portion of Old Asset Sold:

Cash received..	$15,000
Portion sold (12% x $100,000)............................	(12,000)
Gain recognized on portion sold......................	$ 3,000

Filzinger:

New asset ($58,000 + 15,000)...	73,000	
Accumulated depreciation - old asset (balance)	220,000	
Cash..		15,000
Old asset (balance)		278,000

This is an exchange of similar assets and a gain is indicated. The gain of $52,000 ($110,000 fair value of old asset - $58,000 book value) *is not* recognized. The new asset is valued at the book value of the old asset ($58,000) plus the cash given ($15,000).

Problem 10-2

Requirement 1

2003:

Expenditures for 2003:

January 3, 2003	$500,000	x 12/12 =	$500,000
March 31, 2003	600,000	x 9/12 =	450,000
June 30, 2003	800,000	x 6/12 =	400,000
October 31, 2003	600,000	x 2/12 =	100,000

Accumulated expenditures
(before interest) - $2,500,000
Average accumulated expenditures - $1,450,000

Interest capitalized:

$1,450,000 x 10% = $145,000 = Interest capitalized

2004:

January 1, 2004 ($2,500,000 + 145,000)	$2,645,000	x 6/6 =	$2,645,000
January 31, 2004	300,000	x 5/6 =	250,000
March 31, 2004	500,000	x 3/6 =	250,000
May 31, 2004	600,000	x 1/6 =	100,000

Accumulated expenditures
(before interest) - $4,045,000
Average accumulated expenditures - $3,245,000

Interest capitalized:

$2,000,000	x 10.0% x 6/12 =	$100,000	
1,245,000	x 7.25%* x 6/12 =	45,131	
$3,245,000		$145,131	= Interest capitalized

* Weighted-average rate of all other debt:

$5,000,000	x 8% =	$400,000		$580,000	
3,000,000	x 6% =	180,000		————————	= 7.25%
$8,000,000		$580,000		$8,000,000	

Problem 10-2 (concluded)

Requirement 2

Accumulated expenditures 6/30/01, before interest capitalization (above)	$4,045,000
2004 interest capitalized (above)	145,131
Total cost of building	$4,190,131

Requirement 3

2003:

$2,000,000 x 10% =	$ 200,000
5,000,000 x 8% =	400,000
3,000,000 x 6% =	180,000
Total interest incurred	780,000
Less: Interest capitalized	(145,000)
2003 interest expense	$ 635,000

2004:

Total interest incurred	$ 780,000
Less: Interest capitalized	(145,131)
2004 interest expense	$ 634,869

EXERCISES

Exercise 11-1

1. Straight-line:

$$\frac{\$240,000 - 20,000}{8 \text{ years}} = \$27,500 \text{ per year}$$

2. Sum-of-the-years' digits:

Sum-of-the-digits is $\{[8 (8 + 1)] \div 2\} = 36$

2003	$220,000 x 8/36	=	$48,889
2004	$220,000 x 7/36	=	42,778

3. Double-declining balance:

Straight-line rate is 12.5% (1 ÷ 8 years) x 2   = 25% DDB rate

2003	$240,000 x 25%	= $60,000
2004	($240,000 - 60,000) x 25%	= $45,000

4. One hundred fifty percent declining balance:

Straight-line rate is 12.5% (1 ÷ 8 years) x 1.5   = 18.75% rate

2003	$240,000 x 18.75%	= $45,000
2004	($240,000 – 45,000) x 18.75%	= $36,563

5. Units-of-production:

$$\frac{\$240,000 - 20,000}{55,000 \text{ units}} = \$4 \text{ per unit depreciation rate}$$

2003	8,000 units x $4	= $32,000
2004	12,000 units x $4	= $48,000

Exercise 11-2

1. Straight-line:

$$\frac{\$240,000 - 20,000}{8 \text{ years}} = \$27,500 \text{ per year}$$

2003	$27,500 x 8/12	=	$18,333
2004	$27,500 x 12/12	=	$27,500

2. Sum-of-the-years' digits:

Sum-of-the-digits is $\{[8(8+1)]/2\} = 36$

2003	$220,000 x 8/36 x 8/12	=	<u>$32,593</u>

2004	$220,000 x 8/36 x 4/12	=	$16,296
	+ $220,000 x 7/36 x 8/12	=	<u>28,519</u>
			<u>$44,815</u>

3. Double-declining balance:

Straight-line rate is 8% (1 ÷ 8 years) x 2 = 25% DDB rate

2003	$240,000 x 25% x 8/12	=	<u>$40,000</u>

2004	$240,000 x 25% x 4/12	=	$20,000
	+ ($240,000 – 60,000) x 25% x 8/12	=	<u>30,000</u>
			<u>$50,000</u>

or,

2004	($240,000 - 40,000) x 25%	=	<u>$50,000</u>

4. One hundred fifty percent declining balance:

Straight-line rate is 12.5% (1 ÷ 8 years) x 1.5 = 18.75% rate

2003	$240,000 x 18.75% x 8/12	=	<u>$30,000</u>

2004	$240,000 x 18.75% x 4/12	=	$15,000
	+ ($240,000 - 45,000) x 18.75% x 8/12	=	<u>24,375</u>
			<u>$39,375</u>

Or,

2004	($240,000 – 30,000) x 18.75%	=	<u>$39,375</u>

5. Units-of-production:

$$\frac{\$220,000 - 20,000}{55,000 \text{ units}} = \$4 \text{ per unit depreciation rate}$$

| 2003 | 6,000 units x $4 = | $24,000 |
| 2004 | 12,000 units x $4 = | $48,000 |

Exercise 11-3

Requirement 1

$$\text{Depletion per ton} = \frac{\$2,000,000}{1,000,000 \text{ tons}} = \$2.00 \text{ per ton}$$

2003 depletion   = $2.00 x 400,000 tons   = **$800,000**

Requirement 2

Depletion is part of product cost and is included in the cost of the inventory of coal, just as the depreciation on manufacturing equipment is included in inventory cost. The depletion is then included in cost of goods sold in the income statement when the coal is sold.

Exercise 11-4

Requirement 1

a. To record the purchase of a patent.

June 30, 2001
Patent...1,000,000
  Cash... 1,000,000

To record amortization on the patent.

December 31, 2001
Amortization expense ($1,000,000 ÷ 5 years x 1/2)............. 100,000
  Patent... 100,000

December 31, 2002
Amortization expense ($1,000,000 ÷ 5 years).................... 200,000
  Patent... 200,000

---

b. To record the purchase of a franchise.

2003
Franchise... 40,000
  Cash... 40,000

Exercise 11-4 (concluded)

Year-end adjusting entries

Patent: To record amortization on the patent.

December 31, 2003

Amortization expense (determined below) 100,000

   Patent... 100,000

Calculation of annual amortization after the estimate change:
     ($ in thousands)

$1,000	Cost
300	Amortization to date (2001-2002)
700	Unamortized cost (balance in the patent account)
÷ 7	Estimated remaining life
$100	New annual amortization

Franchise: To record amortization of franchise.

December 31, 2003

Amortization expense ($40,000 ÷ 20 years) 2,000

   Franchise.. 2,000

Requirement 2

Intangible assets:

Patent	$600,000	[1]
Franchise	38,000	[2]
Total intangibles	$638,000	

[1] $1,000,000 – 400,000
[2] $40,000 - 2,000

Exercise 11-5

Depreciation expense (determined below)......................... 48,889
   Accumulated depreciation 48,889

Calculation of annual depreciation after the estimate change:

	$640,000	Cost
$60,000		Old annual depreciation ($600,000 ÷ 10 years)
x 3 years	180,000	Depreciation to date (2001-2002)
	460,000	Book value
	20,000	Revised residual value
	440,000	Revised depreciable base
	÷ 9	Estimated remaining life (12 years - 3 years)
	$ 48,889	New annual depreciation

Exercise 11-6

Analysis:

	Correct (Should Have Been Recorded)		**Incorrect** (As Recorded)	
2000 Machine	200,000		Expense	200,000
Cash		200,000	Cash	200,000
2000 Expense	22,500		Depreciation entry omitted	
Accum. deprec.		22,500		
2001 Expense	22,500		Depreciation entry omitted	
Accum. deprec.		22,500		
2002 Expense	22,500		Depreciation entry omitted	
Accum. deprec.		22,500		

During the three-year period, depreciation expense was *understated* by $67,500, but other expenses were *overstated* by $200,000, so net income during the period was *understated* by $132,500, which means retained earnings is currently *understated* by that amount.

During the three-year period, accumulated depreciation was understated, and continues to be understated by $67,500.

To correct incorrect accounts

Machine	200,000	
Accumulated depreciation ($22,500 x 3 years) ...		67,500
Retained earnings ($200,000 – 67,500)..............		132,500

PROBLEMS

Problem 11-1

1. Depreciation for 2001 and 2002.

December 31, 2001
Depreciation expense ($60,000 ÷ 6 years x $^8/_{12}$)................. 6,667
   Accumulated depreciation - equipment 6,667

December 31, 2002
Depreciation expense ($60,000 ÷ 6 years) 10,000
   Accumulated depreciation - equipment 10,000

2. The year 2003 expenditure.

January 4, 2003
Repair and maintenance expense 4,000
Equipment... 11,000
   Cash.. 15,000

3. Depreciation for the year 2003.

December 31, 2003
Depreciation expense (determined below) 8,579
   Accumulated depreciation - equipment 8,579

Calculation of annual depreciation after the estimate change:

$ 60,000	Cost
16,667	Depreciation to date ($5,557 + 10,000)
43,333	Book value
11,000	Asset addition
54,333	New depreciable base
÷ 6 1/3	Estimated remaining life (8 years - 1 2/3 years)
$ 8,579	New annual depreciation

Problem 11-2

Requirement 1

Machine 651:

$$\frac{\$150{,}000 - 10{,}000}{10 \text{ years}} = \$14{,}000 \text{ per year} \times 3 \text{ years} = \qquad \$42{,}000$$

Machine 652:

$$\frac{\$280{,}000}{7 \text{ years}} = \$40{,}000 \text{ per year} \times 2.5 \text{ years} = \qquad 100{,}000$$

Machine 653:

$$\frac{\$110{,}000 - 5{,}000}{8 \text{ years}} = \$13{,}125 \text{ per year} \times 3/12 = \qquad \underline{3{,}281}$$

Accumulated depreciation, 12/31/02 $\qquad$ **$\underline{\underline{\$145{,}281}}$**

Requirement 2

Building:

Useful life of the building:

$$\frac{\$300{,}000}{5 \text{ years}} = \$60{,}000 \text{ in depreciation per year}$$
(1998-2002)

$$\frac{\$1{,}250{,}000 - 50{,}000}{\$60{,}000} = 20\text{-year useful life}$$

Problem 11-2 (concluded)

To record depreciation on the building.

Depreciation expense [($1,250,000 - 50,000) ÷ 20 years]	60,000	
Accumulated depreciation - building..........................		60,000

To record depreciation on the equipment.

Depreciation expense (determined below)	74,725	
Accumulated depreciation - equipment		74,725

Equipment:

Machine 652 (determined above)		$40,000
Machine 653 (determined above)		13,125
Machine 651:		
Cost	$150,000	
Less: Accumulated depreciation	42,000	
Book value, 12/31/02	108,000	
Revised remaining life (8 years - 3 years)	÷ 5 years	21,600
		$74,725

Problem 11-3

Requirement 1

Plant and equipment:

Depreciation to date:

$120 million ÷ 8 years = $15 million per year x 3 years = $45 million

Book value: $120 million – $45 million = $75 million

Purchased technology:

Amortization to date:

$60 million ÷ 6 years = $10 million per year x 3 years = $30 million

Book value: $60 million – $30 million = $30 million

Requirement 2

Tangible operational assets and finite life intangibles are tested for impairment only when events or changes in circumstances indicate book value may not be recoverable.

Requirement 3

Goodwill should be tested for impairment on an annual basis and in between annual test dates if events or circumstances indicate that the fair value of the reporting unit is below its book value.

Requirement 4

Plant and equipment:

An impairment loss is indicated because the book value of the assets, $75 million, is greater than the $65 undiscounted sum of future cash flows. The amount of the impairment loss is determined as follows:

Book value	$75 million
Fair value	(50) million
Impairment loss	25 million

© The McGraw-Hill Companies, Inc., 2004

Problem 11-3 (concluded)

Purchased technology:

An impairment loss is indicated because the book value of the asset, $30 million, is greater than the $15 undiscounted sum of future cash flows. The amount of the impairment loss is determined as follows:

Book value	$30 million
Fair value	(10) million
Impairment loss	20 million

Goodwill:

An impairment loss is indicated because the book value of the assets of the reporting unit, $310 million, is greater than the $300 million fair value of the reporting unit. The amount of the impairment loss is determined as follows:

Determination of implied goodwill:

Fair value of Valpo	$300 million
Fair value of Valpo's net assets (excluding goodwill)	(250) million
Implied value of goodwill	$ 50 million

Measurement of impairment loss:

Book value of goodwill	$80 million
Implied value of goodwill	(50) million
Impairment loss	$30 million

Chapter 12 Investments

Exercise 12-1

Requirement 1

2003

March 1

	($ in millions)	
Investment in Platinum Gems, Inc. shares	124	
Cash		124

April 13

| Investment in Oracle bonds... | 200 | |
| Cash .... | | 200 |

July 20

| Cash .... | 3 | |
| Investment revenue... | | 3 |

October 13

| Cash .... | 10 | |
| Investment revenue... | | 10 |

October 14

Cash	205	
Investment in Oracle bonds.......................................		200
Gain on sale of investments.......................................		5

November 1

| Investment in SPI preferred shares .... | 40 | |
| Cash .... | | 40 |

December 31
Adjusting entries:

Investment in Platinum Gems shares	4	
Unrealized holding gain on investments		
([$64 x 2 million shares] - $124 million)...............................		4

($ in millions)

Unrealized holding loss on investments	
([$74 x 500,000 shares] - $40 million)...	3
Investment in SPI preferred shares	3

2004

January 25

Cash ([2 million shares x $1/2$] x $65)....................................	65
Unrealized holding gain on	
investments ($1/2$ amount from adjusting entry)..............................	2
Gain on sale of investments (difference)..................................	3
Investment in Platinum Gems	
shares ($128 million balance after adjusting entry x $1/2$)	64

March 1

Cash ($78 x 500,000 shares)	39
Loss on sale of investments (difference)	1
Unrealized holding loss on investments (from adjusting entry)..	3
Investment in SPI preferred (balance after adjusting entry)..........	37

Requirement 2

2003 Income Statement

($ in millions)

Investment revenue (from July 20; Oct. 13)..............................	$13
Gain on sale of investments (from Oct. 14)	5

Note: Unlike for trading securities, unrealized holding gains and losses are not included in income for securities available for sale.

Exercise 12-2

1. Investments reported as current assets.

Security	A	$ 725,000
Security	B	200,000
Security	C	560,000
Security	E	970,000
Total		$2,455,000

2. Investments reported as noncurrent assets.

Security	D	$ 865,000
Security	F	412,000
		$1,277,000

3. Unrealized gain (or loss) component of income before taxes.

Trading Securities:

		Cost	Fair value	Unrealized gain (loss)
Security	A	$ 700,000	$ 725,000	$25,000
	B	210,000	200,000	(10,000)
Totals		$ 910,000	$ 925,000	$ 15,000

4. Unrealized gain (or loss) component of shareholders' equity.

Securities Available For Sale:

		Cost	Fair value	Unrealized gain (loss)
Security	C	$ 500,000	$ 560,000	$60,000
	D	850,000	865,000	15,000
Totals		$1,350,000	$1,425,000	$75,000

Exercise 12-3

Purchase   ($ in millions)
Investment in Reed's Restaurant Supplies shares   73
   Cash   73

Net income
Investment in Reed's Rest. Supplies shares (35% x $20million)   7
   Investment revenue   7

Dividends
Cash (35% x 12 million shares x $1.10) 4.62
   Investment in Reed's Restaurant Supplies shares 4.62

Adjusting entry
No entry

Exercise 12-4

Purchase

	($ in millions)
Investment in Conley Trucks	76
Cash	76

Net income

Investment in Conley Trucks shares (25% x $60 million)	15
Investment revenue..	15

Dividends

Cash (5 million shares x $1.20)..	6
Investment in Conley Trucks shares	6

Depreciation Adjustment

Investment revenue ($10 million [calculation below‡] ÷ 5 years)	2
Investment in Conley Trucks shares	2

‡**Calculations:**

	Investee Net Assets ⇓	Net Assets Purchased ⇓	Difference Attributed to: ⇓
Cost		$76	
			Goodwill: $13
Fair value:	$252* x 25% =	$63	
			Undervaluation of assets: $10
Book value:	$212 x 25% =	$53	

*[$212 + 40] = $252

Adjusting entry

No entry

PROBLEMS

Problem 12-1

Requirement 1

Purchase		($ in 000s)
Investment in Austin shares	648	
Cash		648

Net income		
Investment in Austin shares (30% x $320,000)	96	
Investment revenue		96

Dividends		
Cash (20,000 shares x $3)	60	
Investment in Austin shares		60

Depreciation Adjustment		
Investment revenue [calculation below‡] ÷ 8 years)	6	
Investment in Austin shares		6

‡**Calculations:**

	Investee Net Assets ⇓	Net Assets Purchased ⇓	Difference Attributed to: ⇓	
Cost		$648		
			Goodwill:	$120
Fair value:	$1,760* x 30% =$528			
			Undervaluation of assets:	$48
Book value:	$1,600 x 30% =$480			

*[$1,600 + 160] = $1,760

Adjusting entry
  No entry

Problem 12-1 (concluded)

Requirement 2

Purchase

($ in 000s)

Investment in Austin shares 648

   Cash 648

Net income

No entry

Dividends

Cash (20,000 shares x $3) 60

   Investment revenue... 60

Adjusting entry

Unrealized holding loss on investments

  ([20,000 shares x $32] – $648,000).. 8

   Investment in Austin shares 8

Problem 12-2

Requirement 1

	($ in millions)
Purchase	
Investment in Monterrey shares	80.0
Cash	80.0
Net income	
Investment in Monterrey shares (40% x $28 million)	11.2
Investment revenue	11.2
Dividends	
Cash (40% x $6 million)...	2.4
Investment in Monterrey shares	2.4
Inventory	
Investment revenue ($1 million x 40%: all sold in 2003)	.4
Investment in Monterrey shares	.4
Depreciation	
Investment revenue ([$4 million x 40%] ÷ 8 years)	.2
Investment in Monterrey shares	.2

‡**Calculations:**

	Investee Net Assets ⇓	**Net Assets Purchased** ⇓	**Difference Attributed to:** ⇓	
Cost		$80		
			Goodwill:	$16 [plug]
Fair value:	$160* x 40% =	$64		
inventory	(1) x 40%		*Undervaluation of inventory:*	$0.4
plant facilities	(4) x 40%		*Undervaluation of plant:*	$1.6
Book value:	$155 x 40% =	$62		

* $155 + 1 + 4

Problem 12-2 (concluded)

Requirement 2

Investment Revenue

		($ in millions)
		11.2 Share of income
Inventory	.4	
Depreciation	.2	
Balance		**10.6**

Requirement 3

Investment in Monterrey shares

		($ in millions)
Cost	80.0	
Share of income	11.2	
		2.4 Dividends
		.4 Inventory
		.2 Depreciation
Balance	**88.2**	

Requirement 4
$80 million cash outflow from investing activities
$2.4 million cash inflow (dividends) among operating activities

Chapter 13 Current Liabilities

EXERCISES

Exercise 13-1

Requirement 1

Cash	6,000,000	
Notes payable...		6,000,000

Requirement 2

Interest expense ($6,000,000 x 14% x $4/12$)	280,000	
Interest payable		280,000

Requirement 3

Interest expense ($6,000,000 x 14% x $2/12$)	140,000	
Interest payable (from adjusting entry)	280,000	
Notes payable (face amount)	6,000,000	
Cash (total)		6,420,000

Exercise 13-2

1.

Interest rate	Fiscal year-end
13%	December 31

$300 million x 13% x $8/12$ = $26 million

2.

Interest rate	Fiscal year-end
10%	October 31

$300 million x 10% x $6/12$ = $15 million

3.

Interest rate	Fiscal year-end
9%	June 30

$300 million x 9% x $2/12$ = $4.5 million

4.

Interest rate	Fiscal year-end
7%	January 31

$300 million x 7% x $9/12$ = $15.75 million

Exercise 13-3

2003

Jan. 22 No entry is made for a line of credit until a loan actually is made. It would be described in a disclosure note.

Mar. 1

Cash	6,000,000	
Notes payable		6,000,000

June 1

Interest expense ($6,000,000 x 10% x $3/12$).................	150,000	
Notes payable (face amount)	6,000,000	
Cash ($6,000,000 + 150,000)		6,150,000

Nov. 1

Cash (difference)...	5,640,000	
Discount on notes payable ($6,000,000 x 8% x $9/12$).....	360,000	
Notes payable (face amount).....................................		6,000,000

Dec. 31
The effective interest rate is 8.5106% ($360,000 ÷ $5,640,000) x $12/9$. So, properly, interest should be recorded at that rate times the outstanding balance times one-twelfth of a year:

Interest expense ($5,640,000 x 8.5106% x $2/12$).............	80,000	
Discount on notes payable		80,000

However the same results are achieved if interest is recorded at the discount rate times the maturity amount times two-twelfths of a year:

Interest expense ($6,000,000 x 8% x $2/12$)	80,000	
Discount on notes payable		80,000

Exercise 13-3 (concluded)

2004

Aug. 1

Interest expense ($6,000,000 x 8% x $7/12$)*	280,000	
Discount on notes payable		280,000
Notes payable (balance)	6,000,000	
Cash (maturity amount)		6,000,000

* or, ($5,640,000 x 8.5106% x $7/12$) = $280,000

Exercise 13-4

1. **Noncurrent liability: $22 million**
   The current liability classification includes (a) situations in which the creditor has the right to demand payment because an existing violation of a provision of the debt agreement makes it callable and (b) situations in which debt is not yet callable, but will be callable within the year if an existing violation is not corrected within a specified grace period – unless it's *probable* the violation will be corrected within the grace period. In this case, the existing violation is expected to be corrected within 6 months.

2. **Current liability: $9 million**
   The debt should be reported as a current liability because it is payable in the upcoming year, will not be refinanced with long-term obligations, and will not be paid with a bond sinking fund.

3. **Current liability: $15 million**
   The requirement to classify currently maturing debt as a current liability includes debt that is callable by the creditor in the upcoming year – even if the debt is not expected to be called

Exercise 13-5

Requirement 1

This is a loss contingency. There may be a future sacrifice of economic benefits (cost of satisfying the warranty) due to an existing circumstance (the warranted awnings have been sold) that depends on an uncertain future event (customer claims).

The liability is probable because product warranties inevitably entail costs. A reasonably accurate estimate of the total liability for a period is possible based on prior experience. So, the contingent liability for the warranty is accrued. The estimated warranty liability is credited and warranty expense is debited in 2000, the period in which the products under warranty are sold.

Requirement 2

2003 Sales

Accounts receivable	7,500,000	
Sales		7,500,000

Accrued liability and expense

Warranty expense (4% x $7,500,000)	300,000	
Estimated warranty liability		300,000

Actual expenditures

Estimated warranty liability	124,800	
Cash, wages payable, parts and supplies, etc.		124,800

Requirement 3

Warranty Liability

		300,000	Estimated liability
Actual expenditures	124,800		
		175,200	Balance

PROBLEMS

Problem 13-1

Requirement 1

Schilling Motors

Cash 42,000,000

    Notes payable   42,000,000

First Bank

Notes receivable 42,000,000

    Cash   42,000,000

Requirement 2

Adjusting entries (December 31, 2003)

Schilling Motors

Interest expense ($42,000,000 x 12% x $2/12$) 840,000

    Interest payable   840,000

First Bank

Interest receivable 840,000

    Interest revenue ($42,000,000 x 12% x $2/12$)   840,000

Maturity (March 31, 2004)

Schilling Motors

Interest expense ($42,000,000 x 12% x $3/12$) 1,260,000

Interest payable (from adjusting entry) 840,000

Notes payable (face amount) 42,000,000

    Cash (total)   44,100,000

First Bank

Cash (total) 44,100,000

    Interest revenue ($42,000,000 x 12% x $3/12$)   1,260,000

    Interest receivable (from adjusting entry)   840,000

    Notes receivable (face amount)   42,000,000

Problem 13-1 (concluded)

Requirement 3

Issuance of note (November 1, 2003)

Cash (difference)...	39,900,000	
Discount on notes payable ($42,000,000 x 12% x $5/12$)		2,100,000
Notes payable (face amount)...		42,000,000

Adjusting entry (December 31, 2003)

Interest expense ($42,000,000 x 12% x $2/12$).................	840,000	
Discount on notes payable		840,000

Maturity (March 31, 2004)

Interest expense ($42,000,000 x 12% x $3/12$).................	1,260,000	
Discount on notes payable		1,260,000
Notes payable (face amount)...	42,000,000	
Cash		42,000,000

Effective interest rate:

Discount ($42,000,000 x 12% x $5/12$)	$ 2,100,000
Cash proceeds	÷ $39,900,000
Interest rate for 4 months'	5.26315%
	x $12/5$
Annual effective rate	12.63%

Problem 13-2

1. This is a loss contingency. Finley can use the information occurring after the end of the year in determining appropriate disclosure. It is unlikely that Finley would choose to accrue the $36 million loss because the judgment will be appealed and that outcome is uncertain. A disclosure note is appropriate:

Note X: Contingency

In a lawsuit resulting from a dispute with a supplier, a judgment was rendered against Eastern Corporation in the amount of $34 million plus interest, a total of $36 million at January 25, 2004. Finley plans to appeal the judgment. While management and legal counsel are presently unable to predict the outcome or to estimate the amount of any liability the company may have with respect to this lawsuit, it is not expected that this matter will have a material adverse effect on the company.

---

2. No disclosure is required because an IRS claim is as yet unasserted, and an assessment is not *probable*. Even if an unfavorable outcome is thought to be probable in the event of an assessment and the amount is estimable, disclosure is not required unless an unasserted claim is probable.

Problem 13-2 (concluded)

3. This is a gain contingency. Gain contingencies are not accrued even if the gain i probable and reasonably estimable. The gain should be recognized only wher realized.

Though gain contingencies are not recorded in the accounts, they should be disclosed in notes to the financial statements.

Note X: Contingency

Finley is the plaintiff in a pending lawsuit filed against AA Asphalt for damages due to lost profits from rejected contracts and for unpaid receivables. The case is in final appeal. No amount has been accrued in the financial statements for possible collection of any claims in this litigation.

---

4. This is a loss contingency. Finley can use the information occurring after the en of the year in determining appropriate disclosure. Finley should accrue the $5 million loss because the ultimate outcome appears settled and the loss is probable

Loss – litigation...	55,000,000	
Liability - litigation		55,000,000

A disclosure note also is appropriate:

Notes: Litigation

In October 2002, the State of Montana filed suit against the Company, seeking civil penalties and injunctive relief for violations of environmental laws regulating hazardous waste. On February 3, 2004, the Company announced that it had reached a settlement with state authorities on this matter. Based upon discussions with legal counsel, the Company, has accrued and charged to operations in 2003, $55 million to cover the anticipated cost of all violations. The Company believes that the ultimate settlement of this claim will not have a material adverse effect on the Company's financial position.

EXERCISES

Exercise 14-1

Requirement 1

$$\underset{\substack{\text{face} \\ \text{amount}}}{\$50 \text{ million}} \times \underset{\substack{\text{annual} \\ \text{rate}}}{12\%} \times \underset{\substack{\text{fraction of the} \\ \text{annual period}}}{{}^{2}\!/_{12}} = \underset{\substack{\text{accrued} \\ \text{interest}}}{\$1 \text{ million}}$$

Requirement 2

	($ in millions)	
Cash ($47 million plus accrued interest)	48	
Discount on bonds ($50 million – $47 million)	3	
Bonds payable (face amount)...		50
Interest payable (accrued interest determined above)............		1

Exercise 14-2

1. Price of the bonds at January 1, 2003

Interest	$ 12,000,000¥	x	11.46992 *	=	$137,639,040
Principal	$240,000,000	x	0.31180 **	=	74,832,000
	Present value (price) of the bonds				$212,471,040

¥   5% x $240,000,000

*   present value of an ordinary annuity of $1: n=20, i=6%

** present value of $1: n=20, i=6%

2. January 1, 2003

Cash (price determined above) 212,471,040

Discount on bonds (difference) 27,528,960

    Bonds payable (face amount)   240,000,000

3. June 30, 2003

Interest expense (6% x $212,471,040) 12,748,262

    Discount on bonds payable (difference)   748,262

    Cash (5% x $240,000,000)   12,000,000

4. December 31, 2003

Interest expense (6% x [$212,471,040 + 748,262) 12,793,158

    Discount on bonds payable (difference)   793,158

    Cash (5% x $240,000,000)   12,000,000

Exercise 14-3

Requirement 1

Schmidt (Issuer)

Cash (102% x $60 million)...	61,200,000	
Convertible bonds payable (face amount)		60,000,000
Premium on bonds payable (difference).................		1,200,000

Facial Mapping (Investor)

Investment in convertible bonds (10% x $60 million)	6,000,000	
Premium on bond investment (difference)	120,000	
Cash (102% x $6 million)..		6,120,000

Requirement 2

Schmidt (Issuer)

Interest expense ($2,700,000 - $60,000)	2,640,000	
Premium on bonds payable ($1,200,000 ÷ 20)............	60,000	
Cash (4.5% x $60,000,000).......................................		2,700,000

Facial Mapping (Investor)

Cash (4.5% x $6,000,000)	270,000	
Premium on bond investment ($120,000 ÷ 20).......		6,000
Interest revenue ($270,000 - $6,000)		264,000

[Using the straight-line method, each interest entry is the same.]

Requirement 3

Schmidt (Issuer)

Convertible bonds payable (10% of the account balance)	6,000,000	
Premium on bonds payable		
(($1,200,000 - [$60,000 x 11]) x 10%)	54,000	
Common stock ([6,000 x 40 shares] x $1 par)		240,000
Paid-in capital – excess of par (to balance)............		5,814,000

Facial Mapping (Investor)

Investment in common stock (to balance)	6,054,000	
Investment in convertible bonds (account balance) .		6,000,000
Premium on bond investment ($120,000 - [$600 x 11])		54,000

PROBLEMS
Problem 14-1
Requirement 1

	Cash Interest 4.5% x Face Amount	Effective Interest 5% x Outstanding Balance		Increase in Balance	Outstanding Balance
					193,537
1	9,000	.05(193,537) =	9,677	677	194,214
2	9,000	.05(194,214) =	9,711	711	194,925
3	9,000	.05(194,925) =	9,746	746	195,671
4	9,000	.05(195,671) =	9,784	784	196,455
5	9,000	.05(196,455) =	9,823	823	197,278
6	9,000	.05(197,278) =	9,864	864	198,142
7	9,000	.05(198,142) =	9,907	907	199,049
8	9,000	.05(199,049) =	9,951*	951	200,000
	72,000		**78,463**	**6,463**	

* rounded.

Requirement 2

	Cash Interest 4.5% x Face Amount	Recorded Interest Cash plus Discount Reduction		Increase in Balance $6,463 ÷ 8	Outstanding Balance
					193,537
1	9,000	(9,000 + 808) =	9,808	808	194,345
2	9,000	(9,000 + 808) =	9,808	808	195,153
3	9,000	(9,000 + 808) =	9,808	808	195,961
4	9,000	(9,000 + 808) =	9,808	808	196,769
5	9,000	(9,000 + 808) =	9,808	808	197,577
6	9,000	(9,000 + 808) =	9,808	808	198,385
7	9,000	(9,000 + 808) =	9,808	808	199,192*
8	9,000	(9,000 + 808) =	9,808	808	200,000
	72,000		**78,463**	**6,463**	

* rounded.

Problem 14-1 (continued)

Requirement 3

(effective interest)

Interest expense (5% x $196,455)....................................	9,823	
Discount on bonds payable (difference).................		823
Cash (4.5% x $200,000)...		9,000

(straight-line)

Interest expense (9,000 + 808)...	9,808	
Discount on bonds payable (6,463 ÷ 8)		808
Cash (4.5% x $200,000)...		9,000

Requirement 4

By the straight-line method, a company determines interest indirectly by allocating a discount or a premium *equally* to each period over the term to maturity. This is allowed if doing so produces results that are not materially different from the interest method. The decision should be guided by whether the straight-line method would tend to mislead investors and creditors in the particular circumstance.

Allocating the discount or premium equally over the life of the bonds by the straight-line method results in an **unchanging dollar amount** of interest each period. By the straight-line method, the amount of the discount to be reduced periodically is calculated, and the effective interest is the "plug" figure.

Unchanging dollar amounts like these are not produced when the effective interest approach is used. By that approach , the dollar amounts of interest vary over the term to maturity because the **percentage rate** of interest remains constant, but is applied to a changing debt balance.

Remember that the "straight-line method," is not an alternative method of determining interest in a conceptual sense, but is an application of the **materiality concept**. The appropriate application of GAAP, the effective interest method, is by-assed as a practical expediency in situations when doing so has no "material" effect in the results.

Problem 14-1 (concluded)

Requirement 5

The amortization schedule in requirement 1 gives us the answer – $19,728. The outstanding debt balance after the June 30, 2002, interest payment (line 5) is the present value at that time ($197,278) of the remaining payments. Since $20,000 face amount of the bonds is 10% of the entire issue, we take 10% of the table amount.

This can be confirmed by calculating the present value:

Interest	$ 900¥	x	2.72325 *	=	$2,451
Principal	$20,000	x	0.86384 **	=	17,276
	Present value (price) of the bonds				$19,727 (rounded)

¥   4.5% x $20,000
*   present value of an ordinary annuity of $1: n=3, i=5%
**   present value of $1: n=3, i=5%

Problem 14-2

Requirement 1

Interest $ 25,000¥   x   3.16987 *   = $ 79,247

Principal $500,000   x   0.68301 **   =   <u>341,505</u>

    Present value (price) of the note $420,752

¥   5% x $500,000

*   present value of an ordinary annuity of $1: n=4, i=10%

**   present value of $1: n=4, i=10%

Operational assets (price determined above)   420,752

Discount on notes payable (difference)   79,248

    Notes payable (face amount)   500,000

Requirement 2

Dec.31	Cash Interest	Effective Interest		Increase in Balance	Outstanding Balance
					420,752
2003	25,000	.10(420,753)	= 42,075	17,075	437,827
2004	25,000	.10(437,827)	= 43,783	18,783	456,610
2005	25,000	.10(456,610)	= 45,661	20,661	477,271
2006	<u>25,000</u>	.10(477,271)	= <u>47,729*</u>	<u>22,729</u>	500,000
	100,000		**179,248**	**79,248**	

* rounded

Requirement 3

Interest expense (market rate x outstanding balance)..........   45,661

    Discount on notes payable (difference)   20,661

    Cash (stated rate x face amount).....................................   25,000

Problem 14-2 (concluded)

Requirement 4

$$\$420{,}753 \div 3.16987 = \$132{,}735$$

amount	(from Table 6A-4)	installment
of loan	n=4, i=10%	payment

Requirement 5

Dec.31	Cash Payment	Effective Interest 10% x Outstanding Balance	Decrease in Balance Balance Reduction	Outstanding Balance
				420,753
2003	132,735	.10(420,753) = 42,075	90,660	330,093
2004	132,735	.10(330,093) = 33,009	99,726	230,367
2005	132,735	.10(230,367) = 23,037	109,698	120,669
2006	132,735	.10(120,669) = 12,066*	120,669	0
	530,940		110,187	420,753

* rounded

Requirement 6

Interest expense (market rate x outstanding balance)	23,037	
Note payable (difference)	109,698	
Cash (payment determined above)......................................		132,735

Problem 14-3

1. Liabilities at October 31, 2003

Bonds payable (face amount)	$48,000,000
Less: discount	6,000,000
Initial balance, Feb. 28, 2003	$42,000,000
June 30, 2003 discount amortization.......................	80,000*
Oct. 31, 2003 discount amortization	83,200**
Oct. 31, 2003 net bonds payable	$42,163,200
Interest payable **	$1,600,000

2. Interest expense for year ended October 31, 2003

June 30, 2003 interest expense................................	$1,680,000*
October 31, 2003 interest expense	1,683,200**
Interest expense for fiscal 2003..............................	$3,363,200

3. Statement of cash flows for year ended October 31, 2003

Pujols would report the cash inflow of $42,000,000*** from the sale of the bonds as a cash flow from financing activities in its statement of cash flows. The accrued interest portion of the cash receipt was paid on June 30 and is part of the cash outflow from operating activities (below).

The $2,400,000 cash interest paid* is cash outflow from operating activities because interest is an income statement (operating) item.

Problem 14-2 (concluded)

Calculations:

February 28, 2003***

Cash ($42 million plus accrued interest)	42,800,000	
Discount on bonds (difference)	6,000,000	
Bonds payable (face amount)		48,000,000
Interest payable ($48 million x 10% x 2/12)		800,000

June 30, 2003*

Interest expense (6% x $42,000,000 x 4/6)	1,680,000	
Interest payable (balance)	800,000	
Discount on bonds payable (difference)		80,000
Cash (5% x $48,000,000)		2,400,000

October 31, 2003**

Interest expense (6% x [$42,000,000 + 80,000] x 4/6)	1,683,200	
Discount on bonds payable (difference)		83,200
Interest payable (5% x $48,000,000 x 4/6)		1,600,000

Problem 14-4

Requirement 1

Bonds payable (face amount)	100,000,000	
Premium on bonds ($20/40$ x $30,000,000)	15,000,000	
Gain on early extinguishment (to balance)		13,000,000
Cash ($100,000,000 x 102%)......................................		102,000,000

Requirement 2

Bonds payable (face amount)	50,000,000	
Premium on bonds ($10/40$ x $30,000,000)	7,500,000	
Gain on early extinguishment (to balance)		5,000,000
Cash (given)...		52,500,000

Chapter 15 Leases

EXERCISES

Exercise 15-1

(a) Gothic Corporation (Lessee)

June 30, 2003

Rent expense...............................	40,000	
Cash		40,000

December 31, 2003

Rent expense...............................	40,000	
Cash		40,000

(b) HardWhere (Lessor)

June 30, 2003

Cash	40,000	
Rent revenue		40,000

December 31, 2003

Cash	40,000	
Rent revenue		40,000

Depreciation expense ($350,000 ÷ 5 years)	70,000	
Accumulated depreciation		70,000

Exercise 15-2

Present Value of Minimum Lease Payments:

($10,000 x 10.78685*) = $107,866

rental present

payments value

* present value of an annuity due of $1: n=12, i=2%

[i = 2% (8% ÷ 4) because the lease
calls for quarterly payments]

Lease Amortization Schedule

	Rental Payments	Effective Interest 2% x Outstanding Balance			Decrease in Balance	Outstanding Balance
						107,866
1	10,000				10,000	97,886
2	10,000	.02 (97,886)	=	1,957	8,043	89,823
3	10,000	.02 (89,823)	=	1,796	8,204	81,619
4	10,000	.02 (81,619)	=	1,632	8,368	73,251
5	10,000	.02 (73,251)	=	1,465	8,535	64,716
6	10,000	.02 (64,716)	=	1,294	8,706	56,010
7	10,000	.02 (56,010)	=	1,120	8,880	47,130
8	10,000	.02 (47,130)	=	943	9,057	38,073
9	10,000	.02 (38,073)	=	761	9,239	28,834
10	10,000	.02 (28,834)	=	577	9,423	19,411
11	10,000	.02 (19,411)	=	388	9,612	9,799
12	10,000	.02 (9,799)	=	201*	9,799	0
	120,000			**12,134**	**107,866**	

* adjusted for rounding of other numbers in the schedule

Exercise 15-2 (concluded)

January 1, 2003

Leased equipment (calculated above).....................	107,866	
Lease payable (calculated above)		107,866
Lease payable	10,000	
Cash (rental payment).......................................		10,000

April 1, 2003

Interest expense (2% x [$107,866 – 10,000])..............	1,957	
Lease payable (difference)	8,043	
Cash (rental payment).......................................		10,000

July 1, 2003

Interest expense (2% x $89,823: from schedule)........	1,796	
Lease payable (difference)	8,204	
Cash (rental payment).......................................		10,000

October 1, 2003

Interest expense (2% x $81,619: from schedule)........	1,632	
Lease payable (difference)	8368	
Cash (rental payment).......................................		10,000

December 31, 2003

Interest expense (2% x $73,251: from schedule)........	1,465	
Interest payable		1,465
Depreciation expense ($107,866 ÷ 2 years)	53,933	
Accumulated depreciation...............................		53,933

January 1, 2004

Interest payable (from adjusting entry)......................	1,465	
Lease payable (difference)	8,535	
Cash (rental payment).......................................		10,000

Exercise 15-3

Lease Amortization Schedule

	Rental Payments	Effective Interest 2% x Outstanding Balance			Decrease in Balance	Outstanding Balance
						107,866
1	10,000				10,000	97,886
2	10,000	.02 (97,886)	=	1,957	8,043	89,823
3	10,000	.02 (89,823)	=	1,796	8,204	81,619
4	10,000	.02 (81,619)	=	1,632	8,368	73,251
5	10,000	.02 (73,251)	=	1,465	8,535	64,716
6	10,000	.02 (64,716)	=	1,294	8,706	56,010
7	10,000	.02 (56,010)	=	1,120	8,880	47,130
8	10,000	.02 (47,130)	=	943	9,057	38,073
9	10,000	.02 (38,073)	=	761	9,239	28,834
10	10,000	.02 (28,834)	=	577	9,423	19,411
11	10,000	.02 (19,411)	=	388	9,612	9,799
12	10,000	.02 (9,799)	=	201*	9,799	0
	120,000			**12,134**	**107,866**	

* adjusted for rounding of other numbers in the schedule

Exercise 15-3 (concluded)

January 1, 2003

Lease receivable ($10,000 x 12)............................	120,000	
Unearned interest revenue ($120,000 – 107,866)		12,134
Inventory of equipment (lessor's cost)..............		107,866

Cash (rental payment)......................................	10,000	
Lease receivable		10,000

April 1, 2003

Cash (rental payment)......................................	10,000	
Lease receivable		10,000

Unearned interest revenue	1,957	
Interest revenue (2% x [$107866 – 10,000]).........		1,957

July 1, 2003

Cash (rental payment)......................................	10,000	
Lease receivable		10,000

Unearned interest revenue	1,796	
Interest revenue (2% x $89,826: from schedule)...		1,796

October 1, 2003

Cash (rental payment)......................................	10,000	
Lease receivable		10,000

Unearned interest revenue	1,632	
Interest revenue (2% x $81,619: from schedule)...		1,632

December 31, 2003

Unearned interest revenue	1,465	
Interest revenue (2% x $73,251: from schedule)...		1,465

January 1, 2004

Cash (rental payment)......................................	10,000	
Lease receivable		10,000

Exercise 15-4

Requirement 1

Lessor's Calculation of Rental Payments

Amount to be recovered (fair market value) $107,866

Rent payments at the beginning
   of each of eight quarters: ($107,866 ÷ 10.7866**) $10,000

    ** present value of an annuity due of $1: n=12, i=2%

Requirement 2

January 1, 2003

Lease receivable ($10,000 x 12).............................	120,000	
Cost of goods sold (lessor's cost)	90,000	
Sales revenue (fair market value)........................		107,866
Unearned interest revenue ($120,000 – 107,866)		12,134
Inventory of equipment (lessor's cost)..............		90,000
Cash (rental payment)	10,000	
Lease receivable		10,000

April 1, 2003

Cash (rental payment)	10,000	
Lease receivable		10,000
Unearned interest revenue	1,957	
Interest revenue (2% x [$107,866 – 10,000])........		1,957

Exercise 15-5

Present value of periodic rental payments*
        ($205,542 x 7.49236**) $1,540,000
    ** present value of an annuity due of $1: n=13, i=11%

The lease meets at least one (actually 3 of 4 in this case) criteria for classification as a capital lease.

January 1, 2003

Cash (given)...	1,540,000	
Helicopter (carrying value)		1,240,000
Deferred gain on sale-leaseback (difference)		300,000
Leased helicopter (present value of lease payments)...............	1,540,000	
Lease payable (present value of lease payments)...............		1,540,000
Lease payable	205,542	
Cash		205,542

December 31, 2003

Interest expense (11% x [$1,540,000 – 205,542])....................	146,790	
Interest payable		146,790
Depreciation expense ($1,540,000 ÷ 15 years*)....................	102,267	
Accumulated depreciation...		102,267
Deferred gain on sale-leaseback ($300,000 ÷ 20 years).......	15,000	
Depreciation expense		15,000

* The helicopter is depreciated over its remaining useful life rather than the lease term because title transfers to the lessee.

PROBLEMS

Problem 15-1

Requirement 1

Capital lease to lessee;   Direct financing lease to lessor.

Since the present value of minimum lease payments (same for both the lessor and the lessee) is equal to (>90%) the fair value of the asset, the 90% recovery criterion is met.

Calculation of the Present Value of Minimum Lease Payments

Present value of periodic rental payments
$$\$32,629 \times 15.32380^{**} \quad = \quad \$500,000$$
$$\text{(rounded)}$$

** present value of an annuity due of \$1: n=20, i=3%

The 75% of useful life criterion is met also. Both additional lessor conditions are met for a nonoperating lease. There is no dealer's profit because the fair value equals the lessor's cost.

Requirement 2

Pal Learning Systems (Lessee)
January 1, 2003

Leased equipment (calculated above)	500,000	
Lease payable (calculated above).....................................		500,000
Lease payable	32,629	
Cash (rental payment)		32,629

April 1, 2003

Interest expense (3% x [\$500,000 – 32,629])...........................	14,021	
Lease payable (difference)..	18,609	
Cash (rental payment)		32,629

Problem 15-1 (concluded)

Star Leasing (Lessor)
January 1, 2003

Lease receivable ($32,629 x 20)..	652,580	
Unearned interest revenue ($652,580 - 500,000)............		152,580
Inventory of equipment (lessor's cost).........................		500,000
Cash (rental payment)...	32,629	
Lease receivable		32,629

April 1, 2003

Cash (rental payment)...	32,629	
Lease receivable		32,629
Unearned interest revenue	14,021	
Interest revenue (3% x [$500,000 – 32,629]).....................		14,021

Requirement 3

Star Leasing (Lessor)
January 1, 2003

Lease receivable ($32,629 x 20).......................................	652,580	
Cost of goods sold (lessor's cost).....................................	450,000	
Sales revenue (fair market value)		500,000
Unearned interest revenue ($652,580 - 500,000)............		152,580
Inventory of equipment (lessor's cost).........................		450,000
Cash (rental payment)...	32,629	
Lease receivable		32,629

April 1, 2003

Cash (rental payment)...	32,629	
Lease receivable		32,629
Unearned interest revenue	14,021	
Interest revenue (3% x [$500,000 – 32,629]).....................		14,021

Problem 15-2

Requirement 1

Lessor's Calculation of Rental Payments

Amount to be recovered (fair market value) $1,097,280

Less: Present value of the guaranteed
     residual value ($75,000 x .68301*)   (51,225)

Amount to be recovered through periodic rental payments $1,046,055

Rental payments at the beginning
     of each of four years: ($1,046,055 ÷ 3.48685**) $300,000

       *   present value of $1: n=4, i=10%
     ** present value of an annuity due of $1: n=4, i=10%

Requirement 2

The lessee's incremental borrowing rate (12%) is more than the lessor's implicit rate (10%). So, both parties' calculations should be made using a 10% discount rate:

Problem 15-2 (continued)

Application of Classification Criteria

1 Does the agreement specify that ownership of the asset transfers to the lessee?

NO

2 Does the agreement contain a bargain purchase option?

NO

3 Is the lease term equal to 75% or more of the expected economic life of the asset?

NO
{4 yrs < 75% of 6 yrs}

4 Is the present value of the minimum lease payments equal to or greater than 90% of the fair value of the asset?

YES
{\$1,046,055[b] > 90% of \$1,046,055}

[b] See calculation below.

Present Value of Minimum Lease Payments

Present value of periodic rental payments ($300,000 x 3.48685**)	$1,046,055
Plus: Present value of the lessee-guaranteed residual value ($75,000 x .68301*)	51,225
Present value of minimum lease payments	$1,097,280

    *   present value of $1: n=4, i=10%
  ** present value of an annuity due of $1: n=4, i=10%

Problem 15-2 (continued)

(a) By Blair Co. (the lessee)

Since at least one criterion is met, this is a **capital lease** to the lessee. Blair records the present value of minimum lease payments as a leased asset and a lease liability.

(b) By HHH (the lessor)

Since the fair market value equals the lessor's carrying value, there is no dealer's profit, making this a **direct financing lease**.

Requirement 3

December 31, 2003

Blair Co. (Lessee)

Leased equipment (calculated above)	1,097,280	
Lease payable (calculated above).....................................		1,097,280
Lease payable	300,000	
Cash (rental payment)		300,000

HHH (Lessor)

Lease receivable ([$300,000 x 4] + $75,000)	1,275,000	
Unearned interest revenue ($1,275,000 – 1,097,280)		177,720
Inventory of equipment (lessor's cost).........................		1,097,280
Cash (rental payment)	300,000	
Lease receivable..		300,000

Problem 15-2 (continued)

Requirement 4

Since both use the same discount rate and since the residual value is lessee-guaranteed, the same amortization schedule applies to both the lessee and lessor:

Dec. 31	Payments	Effective Interest 10% x Outstanding Balance	Decrease in Balance	Outstanding Balance
		Lease Amortization Schedule		
2003				1,097,280
2003	300,000		300,000	797,280
2004	300,000	.10 (797,280) = 79,728	220,272	577,008
2005	300,000	.10 (577,008) = 57,701	242,299	334,709
2006	300,000	.10 (334,709) = 33,471	266,529	68,180
2007	75,000	.10 (68,180) = 6,820*	68,180	0
	1,275,000	177,720	1,097,280	

Requirement 5
December 31, 2004

Blair Co. (Lessee)

Interest expense (10% x [$1,097,280 - 300,000])....................	79,728	
Lease payable (difference)	220,272	
Cash (rental payment)...		300,000
Depreciation expense ([$1,097,280 - 75,000] ÷ 4 years)	255,570	
Accumulated depreciation......................................		255,570

HHH (Lessor)

Cash (rental payment)..	300,000	
Lease receivable		300,000
Unearned interest revenue	79,728	
Interest revenue (10% x [$1,097,280 - 300,000])		79,728

Problem 15-2 (concluded)

Requirement 6

December 31, 2007

Blair Co. (Lessee)

Depreciation expense ([$1,097,280 - 75,000] ÷ 4 years)	255,570	
Accumulated depreciation		255,570
Interest expense (10% x 68,180: from schedule as rounded)....	6,820	
Lease payable (difference : from schedule)..........................	68,180	
Accumulated depreciation ($1,097,280 - 75,000)	1,022,280	
Loss on residual value guarantee ($75,000 - 4,500).............	71,500	
Leased equipment (account balance)		1,097,280
Cash ($75,000 - 4,500)		71,500

HHH (Lessor)

Inventory of equipment (actual residual value)	4,500	
Cash ($75,000 - 4,500)..	71,500	
Lease receivable (account balance).............................		75,000
Unearned interest revenue (account balance)	6,820	
Interest revenue (10% x 68,180: from schedule as rounded) 6,820		

Chapter 16 Accounting for Income Taxes

EXERCISES

Exercise 16-1

Since taxable income is less than accounting income, a future taxable amount will occur when the temporary difference reverses. This means a deferred tax liability should be recorded to reflect the future tax consequences of the temporary difference.

	($ in millions)	
Income tax expense (to balance)	28.0	
Deferred tax liability ([$80 million – 50 million] x 35%)		10.5
Income tax payable ($50 million x 35%)		17.5

Exercise 16-2

Income tax expense (to balance)	249,000	
Deferred tax asset ($90,000 x 40%)	36,000	
Income tax payable (given)		285,000

Exercise 16-3

Requirement 1

	Current Year 2003	Future Deductible Amounts
	($ in millions)	
Temporary difference:		(280)
Taxable income	720	
Enacted tax rate	40%	40%
Tax payable currently	288	
Deferred tax asset		(112)
		↓
Deferred tax asset:		
Ending balance		$ 112
Less: beginning balance ($300 x 40%)		(120)
Change in balance		$(8)

Journal entries at the end of 2003

Income tax expense (to balance)	296	
Deferred tax asset (determined above)		8
Income tax payable (determined above)		288
Valuation allowance – deferred tax asset	40	
Income tax expense		40

Of course, these two entries can be combined.

Exercise 16-3 *(concluded)*

Requirement 2

	($ in millions)	
Income tax expense (to balance)	296	
Deferred tax asset (determined above)		8
Income tax payable (determined above)		288
Income tax expense	16	
Valuation allowance – deferred tax asset ($[^1/_2 \times \$112] - \$40$)		16

Of course, these two entries can be combined.

Exercise 16-4

Requirement 1

	Current Year 2003	Future Taxable Amounts 2004 2005 2006	Future Taxable Amounts
		($ in thousands)	
Accounting income	900		
Non-temporary difference:			
Municipal bond interest	(160)		
Temporary difference:			
Depreciation	(40)	(8) 8 40	40
Taxable income	700		
Enacted tax rate	40%		40%
Tax payable currently	280		
Deferred tax liability			16
			↓

Deferred tax liability:

Ending balance	$16
Less: beginning balance	0
Change in balance	$16

Journal entry at the end of 2003

Income tax expense (to balance)	296	
Deferred tax liability (determined above)		16
Income tax payable (determined above)		280

Requirement 2

	($ in thousands)
Pretax accounting income	$900
Income tax expense	(296)
Net income	$604

Exercise 16-5

Income Statement
For the fiscal year ended June 30, 2003

	($ in millions)
Revenues	$415
Cost of goods sold	(175)
Gross profit	$240
Operating expenses	(90)
Income from continuing operations before income taxes	$150
Income tax expense	(60)
Income before extraordinary item and cumulative effect of accounting change	$90
Extraordinary casualty loss, less applicable income taxes of $2	(3)
Cumulative effect of change in depreciation methods, less applicable income taxes of $16	(24)
Net income	$63

PROBLEMS

Problem 16-1

Requirement 1

($ in millions)	Current Year 2003	Future Taxable Amounts			Future Taxable Amounts [total]
		2004	2005	2006	
Accounting income	68				
Temporary difference:					
Lot sales	(48)	16	20	12	48
Taxable income	20				
Enacted tax rate	40%				40%
Tax payable currently	8				
Deferred tax liability					19.2
					↓

Deferred tax liability:

Ending balance	$19.2
Less: beginning balance	(0.0)
Change in balance	$19.2

Journal entry at the end of 2003

Income tax expense (to balance)	27.2	
Deferred tax liability (determined above)		19.2
Income tax payable (determined above)		8.0

Problem 16-1 (concluded)
Requirement 2

($ in millions)	Current Year 2004	Future Taxable Amounts 2005 2006	Future Taxable Amounts [total]
Accounting income	60		
Temporary difference:			
Lot sales	16	20 12	32
Taxable income	44		
Enacted tax rate	40%		35%
Tax payable currently	17.6		
Deferred tax liability			11.2
			↓
Deferred tax liability:			
Ending balance			$11.2
Less: beginning balance			(19.2)
Change in balance			$(8.0)

Journal entry at the end of 2004		
Income tax expense (to balance)	9.6	
Deferred tax liability (determined above)	8.0	
Income tax payable (determined above)		17.6

Requirement 3

The balance in the deferred tax liability account at the end of 2004 would have been $12.8 million if the new tax rate had not been enacted:

Future taxable amounts	$32 million
Previous tax rate	40%
Deferred tax liability	$12.8 million

The effect of the change is included in income tax expense, because income tax expense is less than it would have been if the rate had not changed.

Problem 16-2
Requirement 1

($ in 000s)

	Prior Years 2001	Prior Years 2002	Current Year 2003	Future Deductible Amounts [total]
Accounting loss			(540)	
Non-temporary difference:				
Fine paid			20	
Temporary differences:				
Loss contingency			40	(40)
Taxable loss			(480)	
Loss carryback	(300)	(120)	420	
Loss carryforward			60	(60)
			0	(100)
Enacted tax rate	40%	40%	40%	40%
Tax payable (refundable)	(120)	(48)	0	
Deferred tax asset				(40) ↓

Deferred tax asset:

Ending balance	$ 40
Less: beginning balance	(0)
Change in balance	$40

Journal entry at the end of 2003

Receivable – income tax refund ($120 + 48)	168	
Deferred tax asset (determined above)	40	
Income tax benefit (to balance)		208

Requirement 2

($ in 000s)

Operating loss before income taxes		$540
Less: Income tax benefit:		
Tax refund from loss carryback	$168	
Future tax benefits	40	208
Net operating loss		$ 332

Problem 16-2 *(concluded)*

Requirement 3

($ in 000s)	Current Year 2004	Future Deductible Amounts
Accounting income	240	
Temporary differences:		
Loss contingency	(40)	
Operating loss carryforward	(60)	
Taxable income	140	0
Enacted tax rate	40%	40%
Tax payable	56	
Deferred tax asset		0
		↓
Deferred tax asset:		
Ending balance		$ 0
Less: beginning balance		(40)
Change in balance		$(40)

Journal entry at the end of 2004		
Income tax expense (to balance)	.96	
Deferred tax asset (determined above)		40
Income tax payable (determined above)		56

Chapter 17 Pensions

EXERCISES

Exercise 17-1

Requirement 1

	($ in millions)
Service cost	$60
Interest cost	36
Actual return on the plan assets, $27 million	
Adjusted for $3 million gain on the plan assets	(24)
Pension expense	**$72**

Requirement 2

Pension expense (calculated above)	72
Prepaid (accrued) pension cost (difference)	12
Cash (given)	60

Exercise 17-2

	($ in millions)
ABO	$(585)
Plan assets	520
Minimum liability	$ (60)
Less: prepaid pension cost – debit balance	30*
Additional liability needed	$ (90)

* Pension expense (given)	200	
Prepaid (accrued) pension cost (difference)......		10
Cash (given)		190

Prepaid (accrued) pension cost:

Beginning of the year	$40
Reduction from entry above...............................	10
End of year	$30

	($ in millions)
Intangible pension asset	90*
Additional liability (calculated above)	90**

*   The entire $90 million can be added to the intangible asset because its balance will not exceed the unrecognized prior service cost ($150 million)

**   Data indicates no previous balance in the "additional liability" account

This adjustment achieves the objective of providing for a minimum liability of $60 million:

Additional liability – credit balance	$(90)
Prepaid (accrued) pension cost – debit balance	30
Pension liability (reported as a single amount on the balance sheet)	$(60)

PROBLEMS

Problem 17-1

Requirement 1

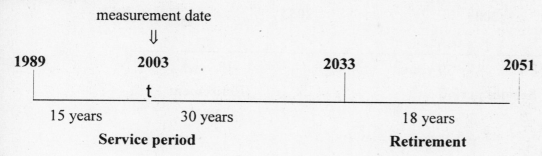

measurement date

⇓

| 1989 | 2003 | 2033 | 2051 |

t

15 years   30 years   18 years

Service period   **Retirement**

Requirement 2

$$1.5\% \times 15 \times \$80,000 = \mathbf{\$18,000}$$

Requirement 3

The present value of the retirement annuity as of the retirement date (end of 2033) is:

$$\$18,000 \times 10.05909^* = \mathbf{\$190,636}$$

* present value of an ordinary annuity of $1: n=18, i=7%

The ABO is the present value of the retirement benefits at the end of 2003:

$$\$190,636 \times .13137^* = \mathbf{\$25,044}$$

* present value of $1: n=30, i=7%

Requirement 4

$$1.5\% \times \mathbf{18} \times \$85,000 = \$22,950$$
$$\$22,950 \times 10.05909^* = \$230,856$$
$$\$230,856 \times .15040^{**} = \mathbf{\$34,721}$$

*   present value of an ordinary annuity of $1: n=18, i=7%

** present value of $1: **n=28**, i=7%

*ternate Exercise and Problem Solutions

17-3

Problem 17-2

Requirement 1

measurement date
$$\Downarrow$$

| 1989 | 2003 | 2033 | 2051 |

|_____|_____t_____|_____|_____|

    15 years   30 years   18 years

       Service period   **Retirement**

Requirement 2

$$1.5\% \times 15 \times \$250{,}000 = \textbf{\$56{,}250}$$

Requirement 3

The present value of the retirement annuity as of the retirement date (end of 2033) is:

$$\$56{,}250 \times 10.05909^* = \textbf{\$565{,}824}$$

    * present value of an ordinary annuity of $1: n=18, i=7%

The PBO is the present value of the retirement benefits at the end of 2003:

$$\$565{,}824 \times .13137^* = \textbf{\$74{,}332}$$

    * present value of $1: n=30, i=7%

Requirement 4

$$1.5\% \times \textbf{18} \times \$250{,}000 = \$67{,}500$$
$$\$67{,}500 \times 10.05909^* = \$678{,}989$$
$$\$678{,}989 \times .15040^{**} = \textbf{\$102{,}120}$$

    *   present value of an ordinary annuity of $1: n=18, i=7%
    ** present value of $1: **n=28**, i=7%

Problem 17-3

Requirement 1

$$1.5\% \times \textbf{14} \times \$250{,}000 = \$52{,}500$$
$$\$52{,}500 \times 10.05909^* = \$528{,}102$$
$$\$528{,}102 \times .12277^{**} = \textbf{\$64{,}835}$$

*   present value of an ordinary annuity of $1: n=18, i=7%

**   present value of $1: **n=31**, i=7%

Requirement 2

$$1.5\% \times 1 \times \$250{,}000 = \textbf{\$3{,}750}$$

Requirement 3

$$\$3{,}750 \times 10.05909^* = \$37{,}722$$
$$\$37{,}722 \times .13137^{**} = \textbf{\$4{,}955}$$

*   present value of an ordinary annuity of $1: n=18, i=7%

**   present value of $1: n=30, i=7%

Requirement 4

$$\$64{,}835 \times 7\% = \textbf{\$4{,}538}$$

Requirement 5

PBO at the *beginning* of 2003 (end of 1999)	$64,835
Service cost:	4,955
Interest cost: $64,835 x 7%	4,538
PBO at the *end* of 2003	$74,228

Note: In requirement 3 of the previous problem this same amount is calculated without separately determining the service cost and interest elements (allowing for a $4 rounding adjustment)

Problem 17-4

Requirement 1

PBO Without Amendment	PBO With Amendment
1.5% x 15 yrs x $250,000 = $56,250	**1.65%** x 15 yrs x $250,000 = $61,875
$56,250 x 10.05909* = $565,824	$61,875 x 10.05909* = $622,406
$565,824 x .13137** = <u>$74,332</u>	$622,406 x .13137** = <u>$81,765</u>

↘ ↙

$7,434
Prior service cost

* present value of an ordinary annuity of $1: n=18, i=7%

** present value of $1: n=30, i=7%

Alternative calculation: 1.65 - 1.5 =   **0.15%** x 15 yrs x $250,000 = $5,625

$5,625 10.05909* = $56,582

$56,582 x .13137** = <u>$7,734</u>

Requirement 2

$7,734 ÷ 20 years (expected remaining service) = <u>**$372**</u>

Requirement 3

1.65% x 1 x $250,000 = $4,125

$4,125 x 10.05909* = $41,494

$41,494 x .14056** = <u>**$5,832**</u>

* present value of an ordinary annuity of $1: n=18, i=7%

** present value of $1: **n=29**, i=7%

Requirement 4

$81,785 x 7% = <u>**$5,725**</u>

Requirement 5

Service cost (from req. 3)	$5,832
Interest cost (from req. 4)	5,725
Return on the plan assets (10% x $170,000)	(17,000)
Amortization of prior service cost (from req. 2)	372
Pension expense	**$5,071**

Problem 17-5

PBO With Previous Rate	**PBO With Revised Rate**
1.5% x 15 yrs x $250,000 = $56,250	1.5% x 15 yrs x $250,000 = $56,250
$56,250 x 10.05909[1] = $565,924	$56,250 x 10.8276[3] = $609,053
$579,404 x .13137[2] = <u>$74,332</u>	$609,053 x .17411[4] = <u>$106,042</u>
↘	↙

$$\$31,710$$
Loss on PBO

[1] present value of an ordinary annuity of $1: n=18, i=7%
[2] present value of $1: n=30, i=7%
[3] present value of an ordinary annuity of $1: n=18, i=6%
[4] present value of $1: n=30, i=6%

Chapter 18 Employee Benefit Plans

Exercise 18-1

	APBO	**Service Cost**
2003	$200,000 x $6/30$ = $\underline{\$40,000}$	$200,000 x $1/30$ = $\underline{\$6,667}$
2004	$216,000 x $7/30$ = $\underline{\$50,400}$	$216,000 x $1/30$ = $\underline{\$7,200}$

30 year attribution period (age 28-57)

Exercise 18-2

	($ in millions)	
Service cost	$61	
Interest cost	12	← (5% x [$210 + 30])
Return on plan assets	(0)	
Amortization of:		
transition obligation	5	←($100 ÷ 20 yrs)
prior service cost	2	←($30 ÷ 15 yrs)
Postretirement benefit expense	$80	

Exercise 18-3

Requirement 1

$25.50   fair value per share
x   12 million   shares granted
= $306 million fair value of award

Requirement 2

no entry

Requirement 3

($ in millions)

Compensation expense ($306 million ÷ 3 years) . 102
    Paid-in capital – restricted stock.................   102

Requirement 4

$25.50   fair value per share
x   12 million   shares granted
x   80%   100% – 20% forfeiture rate
= $244.8 million   fair value of award

Exercise 18-4

Requirement 1

At January 1, 2003, the estimated value of the award is:

    $7   estimated fair value per option
   x 75,000   options granted
   = $525,000   total compensation

Requirement 2

Compensation expense ($525,000 ÷ 5 years)................................ 105,000
   Paid-in capital – stock options   105,000

Requirement 3

Compensation expense (calculated below)................................. 91,875
   Paid-in capital – stock options   91,875

At December 31, 2004, the estimated value of the award is:

   $525,000   total compensation
   x   90%   adjustment for 10% forfeiture
   = $472,500   adjusted total compensation
   -   105,000   expensed previously
     $367,500   to be expensed
   ÷   4 years
   = $91,875   expense in each of last four years

Exercise 18-5

Requirement 1

No liability or deferred compensation because the intrinsic value of the SARs is zero: [$23 − $23] x 48,000 shares = $0

Requirement 2

December 31, 2003   ($ in 000s)

Compensation expense*.....................................   32

    Liability − SAR plan   32

* **Calculation:**

[$25-23] x 48,000	x	$1/3$	−	$0	=	**$32,000**
estimated total compensation		fraction of service to date		expensed earlier		current expense

December 31, 2004

  No entry

* **Calculation:**

[$24-23] x 48,000	x	$2/3$	−	$32,000	=	**0**
estimated total compensation		fraction of service to date		expensed earlier		current expense

December 31, 2005

Compensation expense*.....................................   64

    Liability − SAR plan   64

* **Calculation:**

[$25-23] x 48,000	x	$3/3$	−	$32,000	=	**$64,000**
estimated total compensation		fraction of service to date		expensed earlier		current expense

Exercise 18-5 (concluded)

Requirement 3

Liability – SAR plan 48

    Compensation expense* 48

  * **Calculation:**

[$24-23] x 48,000	x	**all**	–	[$32 + 64]	= $(48,000)
actual		fraction		expensed	current
total		of service		earlier	expense
compensation		to date			

Liability – SAR plan (account balance) 48

    Cash 48

Chapter 19 Shareholders' Equity

EXERCISES
Exercise 19-1

February 13

Cash (60 million shares x $10 per share)	600	
Common stock (60 million shares x $1 par)..................		60
Paid-in capital – excess of par (difference)...................		540

February 14

Legal expenses (1 million shares x $10 per share)	10	
Common stock (1 million shares x $1 par)		1
Paid-in capital – excess of par (difference)..................		9

Note: Because 60 million shares sold the previous day for $10 per share, it's reasonable to assume a $10 per share fair value.

February 14

Cash	90	
Common stock (3 million shares x $1 par)		3
Paid-in capital – excess of par, common*..............		27
Preferred stock (1 million shares x $50 par).................		50
Paid-in capital – excess of par, preferred**............		10

*   3 million shares x [$10 market value - $1 par].

** Since the value of the common shares is known ($30 million), the market value of the preferred ($60 million) is assumed from the total selling price ($90 million).

November 16

Property, plant, and equipment (cash value).................	1,844,000	
Common stock (190,000 shares at $1 par per share).......		190,000
Paid-in capital – excess of par (difference)...............		1,654,000

Exercise 19-2

1. January 8, 2003

($ in millions)

Common stock (8 million shares x $1 par)...............................	8	
Paid-in capital – excess of par (8 million shares x $3*)................	24	
Retained earnings (difference)......................................	16	
Cash (8 million shares x $6 per share)		48

 * Paid-in capital – excess of par: $1,200 ÷ 400 million shares

2. August 24, 2003

Common stock (16 million shares x $1 par)	16	
Paid-in capital – excess of par (16 million shares x $3)	48	
Paid-in capital – reacquired shares (difference)...................		24
Cash (16 million shares x $5.50 per share)		88

3. July 26, 2004

Cash (12 million shares x $7 per share).........................	84	
Common stock (12 million shares x $1 par)		12
Paid-in capital – excess of par (difference)............................		72

Exercise 19-3

Requirement 1

a. February 20 – declaration date

Investment in Brown International stock	15,000	
Gain on appreciation of investment ($500,000 - $485,000)		15,000
Retained earnings (100,000 shares at $5 per share)	500,000	
Property dividends payable		500,000

February 28 – date of record
        no entry

March 20 – payment date

Property dividends payable	500,000	
Investment in Brown International stock		500,000

b. April 4

Paid-in capital – excess of par, common*	180,000	
Common stock (25% x [728,000 - 8,000] shares at $1 par) ..		180,000

   alternatively, retained earnings may be debited.

c. July 25

Retained earnings (27,000* x $12 per share)............................	324,000	
Common stock (27,000* x $1 par)		27,000
Paid-in capital – excess of par, common (difference).....		297,000

  * 3% x [728,000 - 8,000 + 180,000 shares] = 27,000 additional shares

Exercise 19-3 (concluded)

d. December 2 – declaration date
Retained earnings.. 7,600
    Cash dividends payable ($100,000 par x 7.6%)   7,600

December 19 – date of record
    no entry

December 27 – payment date
Cash dividends payable 7,600
    Cash   7,600

e. December 2 – declaration date
Retained earnings.. 463,500
    Cash dividends payable (927,000* x $.50)   463,500

* 728,000 - 8,000 + 180,000 + 27,000 = 927,000 shares

December 19 – date of record
    no entry

December 27 – payment date
Cash dividends payable 463,500
    Cash   463,500

Requirement 2

Paid-in capital:

Preferred stock, 7.6%, 100,000 shares at $1 par	$ 100,000
Common stock, 927,000[1] shares at $1 par	927,000
Paid-in capital – excess of par, preferred	2,900,000
Paid-in capital – excess of par, common	5,275,000 [2]
Retained earnings..	9,488,580 [3]
Treasury stock, at cost; 8,000 common shares	(88,000)
Total shareholders' equity...	**$18,402,580**

[1] 728,000 - 8,000 + 180,000 + 27,000 = 927,000 shares
[2] $5,158,000 - 180,000 + 297,000 = $5,275,000
[3] $9,800,000 - 500,000 - 324,000 - 7,600 - 463,500 + 900,000 = $9,488,580

PROBLEMS

Problem 19-1

Requirement 1

a. March 6, 2003

($ in millions)

Retirement

Common stock (3 million sh. x $1)	3	
Paid-in capital – excess of par		
(3 million shares x $7*)	21	
Paid-in capital – reacquired shares	1	
Retained earnings (plug)	5	
Cash		30

* Paid-in capital – excess of par: $560 ÷ 80

Treasury Stock

Treasury stock (3 million sh. x $10)	30	
Cash		30

b. September 3, 2003

Cash (1 million sh. x $11)	11	
Common stock (1 million sh. x $1)		1
Paid-in capital – excess of par		10

Cash (1 million sh. x $11)	11	
Treasury stock (1 million sh. x $10)		10
Paid-in capital– reacquired sh.		1

c. November 14, 2005

Cash	14	
Common stock (2 million sh. x $1)		2
Paid-in capital – excess of par		12

Cash	14	
Paid-in cap.- reacquired sh.(1 +4)	5	
Retained earnings (plug)	1	
Treasury stock (2 million sh. x $10)		20

Problem 19-1 (concluded)

Requirement 2

Shareholders' Equity		$ in millions
	Retired Stock	**Treasury Stock**
Paid-in capital:		
Common stock, at $1 par, ...	$ 79	$ 80
Paid-in capital – excess of par	561 *	560
Paid-in capital – reacquired shares...................................	0	0
Retained earnings	339 **	349 ***
Less: treasury stock, 1 million shares (at cost)		(10)
Total shareholders' equity	$979	$979

```
*    560 - 21 + 10 + 12
**   350 - 11
***  350 - 1
```

or, alternatively:

Paid-in capital:		
Common stock, at $1 par, ...	$ 79	$ 80
Additional paid-in capital...	561 *	560
Retained earnings	339 **	349 ***
Less: treasury stock, 1 million shares (at cost)		(10)
Total shareholders' equity	$979	$979

```
*    560 - 21 + 10 + 12
**   350 - 11
***  350 - 1
```

Problem 19-2

Requirement 1
a. November 2 – declaration date

Retained earnings	252,000,000	
Cash dividends payable (315 million shares at $.80/share)		252,000,000

November 16 – date of record
        no entry

December 2 – payment date

Cash dividends payable	252,000,000	
Cash		252,000,000

b. March 3 – declaration date

Investment in bonds..	900,000	
Gain on appreciation of investment		
($4.8 million – 3.9 million..		900,000

Retained earnings	4,800,000	
Property dividends payable		4,800,000

March 14– date of record
        no entry

April 6– payment date

Property dividends payable	4,800,000	
Investment in bonds		4,800,000

c. July 13

Retained earnings (15,750,000* x $21 per share)............	330,750,000	
Common stock ([15,750,000* – 750,000] x $1 par) ..		15,000,000
Paid-in capital – excess of par		
([15,750,000* – 750,000] x $20 per share)................		300,000,000
Cash (750,000 shares at $21 market price per share).....		15,750,000

* 5% x 315,000,000 shares = 15,750,000 additional shares

Problem 19-2 (continued)

d. November 2 – declaration date
Retained earnings... 264,000,000
   Cash dividends payable (330,000,000* x $.80)..............   264,000,000
   * 315,000,000 + 15,000,000 = 330,000,000 shares

November 16 – date of record
     no entry

December 2 – payment date
Cash dividends payable 264,000,000
   Cash   264,000,000

e. January 16
Paid-in capital – excess of par 165,000,000
   Common stock (165,000,000* shares at $1 par)   165,000,000

    * 330,000,000 shares x 50% = 165,000,000 shares

f. November 2 – declaration date
Retained earnings.. 321,750,000
   Cash dividends payable (495,000,000 * x $.65).............   321,750,000

   * 315,000,000 + 15,000,000 + 165,000,000 = 495,000,000 shares

November 16 – date of record
     no entry

December 2 – payment date
Cash dividends payable 321,750,000
   Cash   321,750,000

Problem 19-2 (concluded)

Requirement 2

BLT Corporation
Statement of Shareholders' Equity
For the Years Ended Dec. 31, 2003, 2004, and 2005 ($ in 000s)

	Common Stock	Additional Paid-in Capital	Retained Earnings	Total Shareholders' Equity
Jan. 1, 2003	**315,000**	**1,890,000**	**2,910,000**	**5,115,000**
Net income			990,000	990,000
Cash dividends			(252,000)	(252,000)
Dec. 31, 2003	**315,000**	**1,890,000**	**3,648,000**	**5,853,000**
Property dividends			(4,800)	(4,800)
Common stock dividend	15,000	300,000	(330,750)	(15,750)
Net income			1,185,000	1,185,000
Cash dividends			(264,000)	(264,000)
Dec. 31, 2004	**330,000**	**2,190,000**	**4,233,450**	**6,753,450**
3 for 2 split effected in the form of a stock dividend	165,000	(165,000)		
Net income			1,365,000	1,365,000
Cash dividends			(321,750)	(321,750)
Dec. 31, 2005	**495,000**	**2,025,000**	**5,276,700**	**7,796,700**

Chapter 20 Earnings Per Share

EXERCISES

Exercise 20-1

1. EPS in 2003

(amounts in millions, except per share amount)

$$\frac{\begin{array}{c}\text{net}\\\text{income}\\\$1{,}200\end{array}}{\underset{\substack{\text{shares}\\\text{at Jan. 1}}}{606}\quad\underset{\substack{\text{treasury}\\\text{shares}}}{-18\,(^{10}/_{12})}\quad\underset{\substack{\text{treasury shares}\\\text{sold}}}{+18\,(^{2}/_{12})}\quad\underset{\substack{\text{new}\\\text{shares}}}{+72\,(^{1}/_{12})}} = \frac{\$1{,}200}{600} = \$2.00$$

Earnings Per Share

2. EPS in 2004

(amounts in thousands, except per share amount)

$$\frac{\begin{array}{c}\text{net}\\\text{income}\\\$1{,}200\end{array}}{\underset{\substack{\text{shares}\\\text{at Jan. 1}}}{(606\;-18\;+18\;+72)}\quad\underset{\substack{\text{stock dividend}\\\text{adjustment}}}{x\;(2.00)}} = \frac{\$1{,}200}{1{,}356} = \$.88$$

Earnings Per Share

3. 2003 EPS in the 2004 comparative financial statements

(amounts in thousands, except per share amount)

$$\frac{\begin{array}{c}\text{net}\\\text{income}\\\$1{,}200\end{array}}{\underset{\substack{\text{weighted average shares}\\\text{as previously calculated}}}{600}\qquad\underset{\substack{\text{stock dividend}\\\text{adjustment}}}{x\;(2.00)}} = \frac{\$1{,}200}{1{,}200} = \$1.00$$

Earnings Per Share

PROBLEMS

Problem 20-1

1. Net loss per share for the year ended December 31, 2003:

(amounts in millions, except per share amount)

$$\frac{\underset{\substack{\text{net} \\ \text{loss}}}{-\$280} \quad \underset{\substack{\text{preferred} \\ \text{dividends}}}{-\$280^1}}{\underset{\substack{\text{shares} \\ \text{at Jan. 1}}}{1{,}200\,(1.05)} - \underset{\substack{\text{treasury} \\ \text{shares}}}{60\,(^8/_{12})\,(1.05)} \quad + \underset{\substack{\text{new} \\ \text{shares}}}{24\,(^4/_{12})}} = \frac{-\$560}{1{,}226} = (\$.46)$$

↑___ stock dividend ___↑
adjustment

Net Loss Per Share

2. Per share amount of income or loss from continuing operations for the year ended December 31, 2003:

(amounts in millions, except per share amount)

$$\frac{\underset{\substack{\text{operating} \\ \text{income}}}{\$520^2} \quad \underset{\substack{\text{preferred} \\ \text{dividends}}}{-\$280^1}}{\underset{\substack{\text{shares} \\ \text{at Jan. 1}}}{1{,}200\,(1.05)} - \underset{\substack{\text{treasury} \\ \text{shares}}}{60\,(^8/_{12})\,(1.05)} \quad + \underset{\substack{\text{new} \\ \text{shares}}}{24\,(^4/_{12})}} = \frac{\$240}{1{,}226} = \$.19$$

↑___ stock dividend ___↑
adjustment

Income from Continuing Operations Per Share

[1] 40,000 shares x $100 x 7% = $280,000

[2] $800,000 – $280,000 = $520,000

3. 2003 and 2002 comparative income statements:

(amounts in millions, except per share amount)

	2003	2002
Earnings (Loss) Per Common Share:		
Income (loss) from operations before extraordinary items	$ .19	$.71
Extraordinary loss from litigation settlement	(.65)	—
Net income (loss)	($ .46)	$.71

Note: The weighted average number of common shares in 2002 should be adjusted for the stock dividend in 2003 for the purpose of reporting 2002 EPS in subsequent years for comparative purposes:

$$\frac{\underset{\substack{\text{net} \\ \text{income}}}{\$900}}{\underset{\substack{\text{1,200} \\ \text{shares} \\ \text{at Jan. 1}}}{} \quad \underset{\substack{(1.05) \\ \text{stock dividend} \\ \text{adjustment}}}{}} = \frac{\$900}{1,260} \quad \overset{\substack{\text{Earnings} \\ \text{Per Share}}}{= \$.71}$$

Problem 20-2

(amounts in millions, except per share amount)

$$\frac{\overset{\substack{\text{net}\\\text{income}}}{\$1{,}050} \overset{\substack{\text{preferred}\\\text{dividends}}}{-\ \$39}}{\underset{\substack{\text{shares}\\\text{at Jan. 1}}}{300(1.04)} + \underset{\substack{\text{new}\\\text{shares}}}{30\,(^{10}/_{12})\ (1.04)} - \underset{\substack{\text{shares}\\\text{retired}}}{2\,(^{6}/_{12})}} = \frac{\$1{,}011}{337} = \$3.0$$

↑__ stock dividend __↑
adjustment

Problem 20-3

The options issued in 2001 are not considered when calculating 2003 E**
because the exercise price ($34) is not less than the 2003 average market price of $.
(although they would have been considered when calculating 2001 or 2002 EPS if t
average price those years had been more than $34).

The options issued in 2003 do not affect the calculation of 2003 EPS becau**
they were issued at December 31. Options are assumed exercised at the beginning **
the year or when granted, whichever is later — when granted, in this case. So, t
fraction of the year the shares are assumed outstanding is $^0/_{12}$, meaning no increase **
the weighted average shares.

The options issued in 2002 are considered exercised for 4 million shares wh**
calculating 2003 EPS because the exercise price ($24) is less than the 2003 avera**
market price of $32. Treasury shares are assumed repurchased at the average pri**
for diluted EPS:

$$
\begin{array}{rl}
& 4 \text{ million shares} \\
\times & \underline{\$24\quad} \text{ (exercise price)} \\
& \$96 \text{ million} \\
\div & \underline{\$32\quad} \text{ (average market price)} \\
& 3 \text{ million shares}
\end{array}
$$

Problem 20-3 (concluded)

(amounts in millions, except per share amounts)

Basic EPS

$$\frac{\underset{\substack{\text{net} \\ \text{income}}}{\$1,050} \quad \underset{\substack{\text{preferred} \\ \text{dividends}}}{- \$39}}{\underset{\substack{\text{shares} \\ \text{at Jan. 1}}}{300(1.04)} + \underset{\substack{\text{new} \\ \text{shares}}}{30\,(^{10}/_{12})\,(1.04)} - \underset{\substack{\text{shares} \\ \text{retired}}}{2\,(^{6}/_{12})}} = \frac{\$1,011}{337} = \$3.00$$

↑___ stock dividend ___↑
adjustment

Diluted EPS

$$\frac{\underset{\substack{\text{net} \\ \text{income}}}{\$1,050} \quad \underset{\substack{\text{preferred} \\ \text{dividends}}}{- \$39} \qquad \underset{\substack{\text{after-tax} \\ \text{interest savings}}}{+ \$40 - 40\%(\$40)}}{\underset{\substack{\text{shares} \\ \text{at Jan. 1}}}{300\,(1.04)} + \underset{\substack{\text{new} \\ \text{shares}}}{30\,(^{10}/_{12})\,(1.04)} - \underset{\substack{\text{shares} \\ \text{retired}}}{2\,(^{6}/_{12})} + \underset{\substack{\text{exercise} \\ \text{of options}}}{(4-3)} \quad \underset{\substack{\text{contingent} \\ \text{shares}}}{+ 13^{*}} \quad \underset{\substack{\text{conversion} \\ \text{of bonds}}}{+ 12^{**}}} = \frac{\$1,035}{363} = \$2.85$$

↑___ stock dividend ___↑
adjustment

* The contingently issuable shares are considered issued when calculating diluted EPS because the condition for issuance (RW net income > $250 million) currently is being met.

** The bonds are considered converted when calculating diluted EPS: 400,000 bonds x 30 shares = 12 million shares upon conversion. Interest = $400 million x 10% = $40 million.

Problem 20-4

(amounts in millions, except per share amounts)

Basic EPS

$$\frac{\underset{\substack{\text{net} \\ \text{income}}}{\$1,300} \quad \underset{\substack{\text{preferred} \\ \text{dividends}}}{-\$80^*}}{\underset{\substack{\text{shares} \\ \text{at Jan. 1}}}{880} \quad \underset{\substack{\text{new} \\ \text{shares}}}{+32\,(^3/_{12})}} = \frac{\$1,220}{888} = \$1.37$$

Diluted EPS

$$\frac{\underset{\substack{\text{net} \\ \text{income}}}{\$1,300} \ \underset{\substack{\text{preferred} \\ \text{dividends}}}{-\$80^*} \qquad\qquad\qquad\qquad \underset{\substack{\text{preferred} \\ \text{dividends}}}{+80^*}}{\underset{\substack{\text{shares} \\ \text{at Jan. 1}}}{880} \ \underset{\substack{\text{new} \\ \text{shares}}}{+32\,(^3/_{12})} \ \underset{\substack{\text{exercise} \\ \text{of options}}}{+(40-30^{**})} \ \underset{\substack{\text{conversion} \\ \text{of preferred} \\ \text{shares}}}{+80}} = \frac{\$1,300}{978} = \$1.33$$

* 8 million shares x $100 par x 10% = $80 million

**Assumed purchase of treasury shares

$$\begin{array}{ll} & \text{40 million shares} \\ \text{x} & \underline{\quad\$30\quad} \ \text{(exercise price)} \\ & \$1,200 \text{ million} \\ \div & \underline{\quad\$40\quad} \text{(average market price)} \\ & \text{30 million shares} \end{array}$$

EXERCISES

Exercise 21-1
Cumulative effect:

SYD depreciation	SL depreciation

$$\left(\frac{10+9+8}{55} \times [\$105,000 - 6,000]\right) - (^3/_{10} \times [\$105,000 - 6,000]) =$$

$$\$48,600 \quad - \quad \$29,700 \quad = \$18,900$$

Accumulated depreciation.. 18,900
    Cumulative effect of accounting change................................ 18,900

Adjusting entry (2003 depreciation):

Depreciation expense ($99,000 ÷ 10 years).. 9,900
    Accumulated depreciation.. 9,900

Exercise 21-2
Requirement 1
To record the change:
Cumulative effect of accounting change 24,600
    Inventory ($96,000 – 71,400) 24,600

Requirement 2
    The cumulative income effect is reported as a separate item of income between extraordinary items and net income. The effect of the change on certain key income numbers should be disclosed for the current period and on a "pro forma" basis for the financial statements of all prior periods that are included for comparison with the current financial statements. Also, the nature of and justification for the change should be described in the disclosure notes.

Exercise 21-3

Requirement 1

Accrued liability and expense

Warranty expense (4% x $720,000)...	28,800	
Estimated warranty liability		28,800

Actual expenditures (summary entry)

Estimated warranty liability	17,600	
Cash, wages payable, parts and supplies, etc.		17,600

Requirement 2

Actual expenditures (summary entry)

Estimated warranty liability ($15,000 – $4,600)........................	10,400	
Loss on product warranty (4% – 3%] x $500,000)	5,000	
Cash, wages payable, parts and supplies, etc.		15,400*

*(4% x $500,000) – $4,600 = $10,400

PROBLEMS

Problem 21-1

a. This is a change in estimate.

No entry is needed to record the change

2003 adjusting entry:
Warranty expense (3% x $800,000) 24,000
    Estimated warranty liability 24,000

A disclosure note should describe the effect of a change in estimate on income before extraordinary items, net income, and related per-share amounts for the current period.

This is a change in estimate.

No entry is needed to record the change

2003 adjusting entry:
Depreciation expense (determined below) 112,500
    Accumulated depreciation 112,500

Calculation of annual depreciation after the estimate change:

$4,000,000	Cost
100,000	Old depreciation ($4,000,000 ÷ 40 years)
x 3 yrs (300,000)	Depreciation to date (2000-2002)
$ 3,700,000	Undepreciated cost
(2,800,000)	New estimated salvage value
$ 900,000	To be depreciated
÷ 8	Estimated remaining life (8 years: 2003-2010)
$ 112,500	New annual depreciation

A disclosure note should describe the effect of a change in estimate on income before extraordinary items, net income, and related per-share amounts for the current period.

Problem 21-1 (continued)

c. This is a change in accounting principle that is reported prospectively.

No entry is needed to record the change.

When a company changes *to the LIFO inventory method* from another inventor[y] method, accounting records usually are insufficient to determine the cumulativ[e] income effect of the change or to determine pro forma disclosures for prior years. S[o] a company changing to LIFO does not report the cumulative income effect in curren[t] income nor revise the balance in retained earnings. Instead, the base year inventor[y] for all future LIFO calculations is the beginning inventory in the year the LIF[O] method is adopted ($13 million in this case). The only disclosure required is [a] footnote to the financial statements describing the nature of and justification for th[e] change as well as an explanation as to why the cumulative income effect was omitte[d].

d. This is a change in accounting principle.

To record the change:

Accumulated depreciation (determined below)	216,000	
Deferred tax liability ($216,000 x 40%)		86,400
Cumulative effect of accounting change (net effect)		129,600

Cumulative effect of the change: ($ in 000s)

	SYD	Straight-line
1999 depreciation	$180 ($990 x $^{10}/_{55}$)	$99 ($990 ÷ 10)
2000 depreciation	162 ($990 x $^{9}/_{55}$)	99 ($990 ÷ 10)
2001 depreciation	144 ($990 x $^{8}/_{55}$)	99 ($990 ÷ 10)
2002 depreciation	126 ($990 x $^{7}/_{55}$)	99 ($990 ÷ 10)
Accumulated depreciation and 1999-2002 reduction in income	$612	$396

$$\searrow \quad \text{difference} \quad \swarrow$$
$$\underline{\$216}$$

2003 adjusting entry:

Depreciation expense ($990,000 ÷ 10 years)	99,000	
Accumulated depreciation		99,000

Problem 21-1 (concluded)

Tax depreciation (MACRS) would have been more than SYD depreciation during the four previous years, but the temporary difference would have been still more if accounting income had been based on straight-line depreciation. As a result, the deferred tax liability is increased from what it was to what it would have been if straight-line depreciation had been used the four previous years. It's not necessary to know what the old or new balance is – only that the new balance should be $86,400 higher.

The cumulative income effect is reported as a separate item of income between extraordinary items and net income. The effect of the change on certain key income numbers should be disclosed for the current period and on a "pro forma" basis for the financial statements of all prior periods that are included for comparison with the current financial statements. Also, the nature of and justification for the change should be described in the disclosure notes.

e. This is a change in estimate.

To revise the liability on the basis of the new estimate:		
Loss – litigation	5,000,000	
Liability - litigation ($45 million – 40 million)		5,000,000

A disclosure note should describe the effect of a change in estimate on income before extraordinary items, net income, and related per-share amounts for the current period.

f. This is a change in accounting principle.

Because the change will be effective only for assets placed in service after the date of change, there would be no cumulative effect on prior years' earnings because the change doesn't affect assets depreciated in prior periods.

The nature of and justification for the change should be described in the disclosure notes. Also, the effect of the change on the current period's income before extraordinary items, net income, and related per-share amounts should be disclosed.

Problem 21-2

a. To correct the error:

Equipment (cost)	9,000	
Accumulated depreciation ([$9,000 ÷ 5] x 2 years))		3,600
Retained earnings ($9,000 – [$1,800 x 2 years))..................................		5,400

2003 adjusting entry:

Depreciation expense ($9,000 ÷ 5)	1,800	
Accumulated depreciation		1,800

b. To reverse erroneous entry:

Cash	51,000	
Office supplies		51,000

To record correct entry:

Storage boxes	51,000	
Cash		51,000

c. To correct the error:

Inventory	112,000	
Retained earnings		112,000

d. To correct the error:

Retained earnings ([$10 x 4,000 shares] – $4,000)	36,000	
Paid-in capital – excess of par		36,000

Note: A "small" stock dividend (<25%) requires that the market value of the additional shares be "capitalized.".

e. To correct the error:

Retained earnings (overstatement of 2002 income).........................	120,000	
Interest expense (overstatement of 2003 interest)		120,000

2003 adjusting entry:

Interest expense ($^4/_6$ x $180,000)...	120,000	
Interest payable ($^4/_6$ x $180,000)		120,000

f. To correct the error:

Prepaid insurance ($216,000 ÷ 3 yrs x 2 years: 2003-2004)	144,000	
Retained earnings ($216,000 – [$216,000 ÷ 3 years])		144,000

2003 adjusting entry:

Insurance expense ($216,000 ÷ 3 years)	72,000	
Prepaid insurance		72,000

EXERCISES
Exercise 22-1

Situation	Cost of goods sold	Inventory	Accounts payable increase (decrease)	Cash paid to suppliers increase (decrease)
1	600	0	0	**600**

1. Summary Entry		
Cost of goods sold	600	
Cash (paid to suppliers of goods)		**600**

Situation	Cost of goods sold	Inventory	Accounts payable increase (decrease)	Cash paid to suppliers increase (decrease)
2	600	18	0	**618**

2. Summary Entry		
Cost of goods sold	600	
Inventory	18	
Cash (paid to suppliers of goods)		**618**

Situation	Cost of goods sold	Inventory	Accounts payable increase (decrease)	Cash paid to suppliers increase (decrease)
3	600	0	558	**558**

3. Summary Entry		
Cost of goods sold	600	
Accounts payable		42
Cash (paid to suppliers of goods)		**558**

Situation	Cost of goods sold	Inventory	Accounts payable increase (decrease)	Cash paid to suppliers increase (decrease)
4	600	18	42	**576**

4. Summary Entry		
Cost of goods sold	600	
Inventory	18	
Accounts payable		42
Cash (paid to suppliers of goods)		**576**

Situation	Cost of goods sold	Inventory	Accounts payable increase (decrease)	Cash paid to suppliers increase (decrease)
5	600	(18)	(42)	**624**

5. Summary Entry		
Cost of goods sold	600	
Accounts payable	42	
Inventory		18
Cash (paid to suppliers of goods)		**624**

Exercise 22-2

RECONCILIATION OF NET INCOME TO
NET CASH FLOWS FROM OPERATING ACTIVITIES

	($ in millions)
Net income	$ 78
Adjustments for noncash effects:	
Increase in accounts receivable	(162)
Increase (decrease) in inventory	0
Increase in accounts payable	29
Increase in salaries payable	12
Decrease in prepaid insurance	18
Depreciation expense	33
Depletion expense	15
Decrease in bond discount	3
Gain on sale of equipment	(75)
Loss on sale of land	24
Increase in income tax payable	36
Net cash flows from operating activities	$ 21

Exercise 22-3

Requirement 1:

a. Summary Entry	Cash (received from customers)	933	
	Accounts receivable		18
	Sales revenue		915

b. Summary Entry	Cost of goods sold	555	
	Inventory	39	
	Accounts payable	24	
	Cash (paid to suppliers of goods)		**618**

c. Summary Entry	Salaries expense	123	
	Salaries payable		15
	Cash (paid to employees)		**108**

d. Summary Entry	Insurance expense	57	
	Prepaid insurance		27
	Cash (paid for insurance)		**30**

e. Summary Entry	Income tax expense	66	
	Income tax payable		60
	Cash (paid for income taxes)		**6**

Depreciation expense and the loss on sale of land are not cash outflows.

Requirement 2:

Cash Flows from Operating Activities:

Cash received from customers	$933
Cash paid to suppliers	(618)
Cash paid to employees	(108)
Cash paid for insurance	(30)
Cash paid for income taxes	(6)
Net cash flows from operating activities	$171

Exercise 22-4

RECONCILIATION OF NET INCOME TO
NET CASH FLOWS FROM OPERATING ACTIVITIES

Net loss	$ (25,000)
Adjustments for noncash effects:	
Depreciation expense	30,000
Increase in salaries payable	2,500
Decrease in accounts receivable	10,000
Increase in inventory	(11,500)
Amortization of patent	1,500
Reduction in discount on bonds	1,000
Net cash flows from operating activities	$8,500

PROBLEMS

Problem 22-1

Classifications

+ I	Investing activity (cash inflow)
− I	Investing activity (cash outflow
+ F	Financing activity (cash inflow)
− F	Financing activity (cash outflow)
N	Noncash investing and financing activity
X	Not reported as an investing and/or a financing activity

Transactions

Example __+ I__ 1. Sale of a building

__+F__ 2. Issuance of preferred stock for cash

__- F__ 3. Retirement of preferred stock

__N__ 4. Conversion of bonds to common stock

__N__ 5. Lease of a machine by capital lease

__+ I__ 6. Sale of a trademark

__- I__ 7. Purchase of land for cash

__N__ 8. Issuance of common stock for a building

__+ I__ 9. Collection of a note receivable (principal amount)

__+F__ 10. Sale of bonds payable

__X__ 11. Distribution of a stock dividend

__N__ 12. Payment of property dividend

__- F__ 13. Payment of cash dividends

__+F__ 14. Issuance of a short-term note payable for cash

__+F__ 15. Issuance of a long-term note payable for cash

__- I__ 16. Purchase of investment securities (not cash equivalent)

__- F__ 17. Repayment of a note payable

__X__ 18. Cash payment for 3-year insurance policy

__+ I__ 19. Sale of land

__N__ 20. Issuance of note payable for land

__- I__ 21. Purchase of common stock issued by another corporation

__N__ 22. Repayment of long-term debt by issuing common stock

__X__ 23. Restriction of retained earnings for plant expansion

__X__ 24. Payment of semiannual interest on notes payable

__- F__ 25. Purchase of treasury stock

__- I__ 26. Loan to a subsidiary

__X__ 27. Sale of merchandise to customers

__X__ 28. Purchase of treasury bills (cash equivalents)

Problem 22-2

A2Z Industries
Spreadsheet for the Statement of Cash Flows

	Dec.31 2002	Changes Debits		Changes Credits		Dec. 31 2003
Balance Sheet						
Assets:						
Cash	1,125	(14) 675				1,800
Accounts receivable	1,350	(1) 450				1,800
Inventory	1,575	(4)1,125				2,700
Land	1,800	(2) 450	X	(3)	225	2,025
Building	2,700					2,700
Less: Acc. depreciation	(810)			(5)	90	(900)
Equipment	6,750	(11)2,700		(7)	900	8,550
Less: Acc. depreciation	(1,440)	(7) 810		(6)	945	(1,575)
Patent	4,500			(8)	900	3,600
	17,550					20,700
Liabilities:						
Accounts payable	1,350			(4)	900	2,250
Accrued expenses	675			(9)	225	900
Lease liability – land	0		X	(2)	450	450
Shareholders' Equity:						
Common stock	9,000			(12)	450	9,450
Paid-in capital-ex. of par	2,025			(12)	225	2,250
Retained earnings	4,500	(12) 675		(10)2,925		
		(13)1,350				5,400
	17,550					20,700
Income Statement						
Revenues:						
Sales revenue				(1)7,935		7,935
Gain on sale of land				(3)	270	270
Expenses:						
Cost of goods sold		(4)1,800				1,800
Depreciation expense-build.		(5) 90				90
Depreciation expense-equip.		(6) 945				945
Loss on sale of equipment		(7) 45				45
Amortization of patent		(8) 900				900
Operating expenses		(9)1,500				1,500
Net income		(10)2,925				**2,925**

Problem 22-2 (continued)

Spreadsheet for the Statement of Cash Flows
(continued)

	Dec.31 2002	Changes Debits	Changes Credits	Dec. 31 2003
Statement of Cash Flows				
Operating activities:				
Cash inflows:				
From customers		(1)7,485		
Cash outflows:				
To suppliers of goods			(4)2,025	
For operating expenses			(9)1,275	
Net cash flows				4,185
Investing activities:				
Purchase of equipment			(11)2,700	
Sale of land		(3) 495		
Sale of equipment		(7) 45		
Net cash flows				(2,160)
Financing activities:				
Payment of cash dividends			(13)1,350	
Net cash flows				(1,350)
Net increase in cash			(14) 675	675
Totals		**24,465**	**24,465**	

X Noncash investing and financing activity

Problem 22-2 (concluded)

A2Z Industries
Statement of Cash Flows
For year ended December 31, 2003 ($ in 000)

Cash flows from operating activities:
Cash inflows:
  From customers $7,485
Cash outflows:
  To suppliers of goods   (2,025)
  For operating expenses   (1,275)
Net cash flows from operating activities $4,185

Cash flows from investing activities:
  Purchase of equipment $ (2,700)
  Sale of land   495
  Sale of equipment   45
Net cash flows from investing activities   (2,160)

Cash flows from financing activities:
  Payment of cash dividends $ (1,350)
Net cash flows from financing activities   (1,350)

  Net increase in cash $ 675

Cash balance, January 1   1,125
Cash balance, December 31 $1,800

Noncash investing and financing activities:

Land acquired by capital lease $450

Problem 22-3

A2Z Industries
Spreadsheet for the Statement of Cash Flows

	Dec.31 2002	Changes Debits		Changes Credits		Dec. 31 2003
Balance Sheet						
Assets:						
Cash	1,125	(15) 675				1,800
Accounts receivable	1,350	(7) 450				1,800
Inventory	1,575	(8)1,125				2,700
Land	1,800	(11) 450	X	(2) 225		2,025
Building	2,700					2,700
Less: Acc. depreciation	(810)			(3) 90		(900)
Equipment	6,750	(12)2,700		(5) 900		8,550
Less: Acc. depreciation	(1,440)	(5) 810		(4) 945		(1,575)
Patent	4,500			(6) 900		3,600
	17,550					20,700
Liabilities:						
Accounts payable	1,350			(9) 900		2,250
Accrued expenses	675			(10) 225		900
Lease liability–land	0			X(11) 450		450
Shareholders' Equity:						
Common stock	9,000			(13) 450		9,450
Paid-in capital-ex. of par	2,025			(13) 225		2,250
Retained earnings	4,500	(13) 675		(1)2,925		
		(14)1,350				5,400
	17,550					20,700

X Noncash investing and financing activity

Problem 22-3 (continued)

Spreadsheet for the Statement of Cash Flows
(continued)

	Dec.31 2002	Changes Debits	Credits	Dec. 31 2003
Statement of Cash Flows				
Operating activities:				
Net income		(1)2,925		
Adjustments for noncash effects:				
Gain on sale of land			(2) 270	
Depreciation expense-build		(3) 90		
Depreciation expense-equip		(4) 945		
Loss on sale of equipment		(5) 45		
Amortization of patent		(6) 900		
Increase in accounts receivable			(7) 450	
Increase in inventory			(8)1,125	
Increase in accounts payable		(9) 900		
Increase in accrued expenses		(10) 225		
Net cash flows				4,185
Investing activities:				
Purchase of equipment			(12)2,700	
Sale of land		(2) 495		
Sale of equipment		(5) 45		
Net cash flows				(2,160)
Financing activities:				
Payment of cash dividends			(14)1,350	
Net cash flows				(1,350)
Net increase in cash			(15) 675	675
Totals		14,805	14,805	

Intermediate Accounting, 3/e

Problem 22-3 (concluded)

A2Z Industries
Statement of Cash Flows
For year ended December 31, 2003 ($ in 000)

Cash flows from operating activities:

Net income	$ 2,925	
Adjustments for noncash effects:		
Gain on sale of land	(270)	
Depreciation expense – building	90	
Depreciation expense – equipment	945	
Loss on sale of equipment	45	
Amortization of patent	900	
Increase in accounts receivable	(450)	
Increase in inventory	(1,125)	
Increase in accounts payable	900	
Increase in accrued expenses	225	
Net cash flows from operating activities		$4,185

Cash flows from investing activities:

Purchase of equipment	$(2,700)	
Sale of land	495	
Sale of equipment	45	
Net cash flows from investing activities		(2,160)

Cash flows from financing activities:

Payment of cash dividends	$(1,350)	
Net cash flows from financing activities		(1,350)

Net increase in cash		$ 675
Cash balance, January 1		1,125
Cash balance, December 31		$1,800

Noncash investing and financing activities:

Land acquired by capital lease		$450